SIMPLE
GARDEN
PROJECTS

SIMPLE GARDEN PROJECTS

A COLLECTION OF ORIGINAL DESIGNS TO BUILD IN YOUR GARDEN

DAVID STEVENS

The Globe Pequot Press

CHESTER, CONNECTICUT

This American edition first published 1992 by
The Globe Pequot Press
Chester, Connecticut 06412

First published in Great Britain in 1992 by
Conran Octopus Limited
37 Shelton Street
London WC2H 9HN

Project Editor: Simon Willis
Art Editor: Karen Bowen
Illustrator: Tom Lomax
Copy Editor: Rebecca Reid
Editorial Assistant: Olivia Aarons
Picture Researcher: Abigail Ahern
Production Controller: Julia Golding

Library of Congress Cataloging-in-Publication Data
Stevens, David, 1943–
    Simple garden projects : a collection of original
designs to build in your garden / David Stevens.
        p.   cm.
    ISBN 1-56440-034-4
    1. Garden ornaments and furniture—Design and construction.
  I. Title.
SB473.5.S74   1992
684.1'8—dc20   91-42560
                              CIP

PUBLISHER'S NOTE
Whilst every effort has been made to
ensure that all the information contained
in this book is correct, the publisher
cannot be held responsible for any loss,
damage, or injury caused by reliance upon
the accuracy of such information. It is also
important to obtain specialist advice on
plumbing and electricity before attempting
any alterations to these services yourself.

DIMENSIONS
Never mix imperial and metric
dimensions when you are making a
calculation or building a project.

Typeset by Servis Filmsetting Ltd,
Manchester
Printed and bound in China

First Edition/First Printing

CONTENTS

INTRODUCTION

Good design is all about simplicity, common sense and, above all, practicality. This is particularly true when designing a yard, as overcomplication is the death of any worthwhile composition. The trouble, of course, is that garden center displays, press reports, and a wealth of expert advice continually tempt us to buy new products and try new ideas, so it's little wonder that this valuable space around our home becomes a jumble of unrelated features.
A well-laid-out yard should fulfill two broad criteria: it must look good for 365 days of the year and must never be a burden, in terms of maintenance, to its owner.
With careful planning, you can produce a yard that is aesthetically pleasing and fits you in an entirely unique way. This planning starts with a simple survey of your plot, moves on to an analysis of what you need, and finishes with the implementation of those ideas.

In this trouble-free yard, maintenance has been kept to an absolute minimum by the clever use of paving, gravel, and planting. The raised terrace is a natural focal point, leading both feet and eye to a secluded sitting area.

PLANNING A YARD

The problem with many a plot comes down to lack of planning. While many people are quite happy to tackle interior decoration and planning, their ideas often tend to dry up as soon as they move outside. In part this is due to the confusion of all those long, Latin plant names, in part to sporadic binges at the local garden center, when we return home with a carload of goodies and little idea of where to put them all. But the real problem is that many of us still look upon the yard as separate from the house, a different environment for a different range of activities. As soon as we realize that the two elements, house and yard, are in fact one, the whole problem becomes a lot simpler.

For a yard to be a success, the layout should be thought about in much the same way as a room inside the house. True, it may not have a ceiling, but the floors and walls are just the same, and you will need furnishings and space for sitting, dining, play, and other activities, as well as the growing of plants. Arches and pergolas are the equivalent of doors; overhead beams and arbours help to define intimate areas; while water, something that is little used inside, can be enjoyed for its almost endless variety as well as its cooling influence.

I have been planning gardens for many years and have learned that, while the genius of creativity flares from time to time, the real worth of a designer is that he or she works to a well-tried and tested set of rules that the designer knows will be successful for any given situation that may arise. In fact, the whole design process is a sequential one and while you may have the glimmer of an idea right at the beginning, the initial stages are all to do with simple fact-finding and information-gathering.

THE SURVEY

Long before you start to work out what you want to see in your yard, you need to know just what features you have got to start with. A simple survey involves measuring the plot, noting down all the existing features, and checking any other relevant factors that are likely to affect the actual design. For this you will need several sheets of paper, a clip board, a pencil, a 100ft. (30m) tape

Above: *A great deal of backyard design is about dividing a large space into a number of more manageable smaller areas. Arches and pergolas are ideal for doing this but should always be positioned so that they form a positive doorway or entrance to the room beyond. This arch does just that as well as providing a slight air of mystery by partially screening the view and heightening tension. Planting is the perfect foil to the old stone path, softening the hard edges of the walkway.*

Opposite: *In this tiny town yard the pattern has been built up by a combination of rectangular shapes close to the house and a strong circle of granite setts further away. The two elements are quite different in character but the broad step effectively separates them and allows the composition to work. As well as providing privacy, walls like this act as the perfect host for climbers, softening what would otherwise be a stark and uninteresting outlook.*

measure, a couple of bamboo canes or metal pins, and a child's magnetic compass. If your yard is so complicated by steep changes of levels, awkward cross-falls, and innumerable trees that you pale at the thought of carrying out the survey yourself, the modest fee charged by a professional surveyor may be well worth the time and trouble you are saved.

The first stage of the survey is to go into the yard and simply draw out the shape of the house and the boundaries to scale, showing the position of doors and windows, manholes or drains, garden buildings and any slope or change of level. The positions of any existing trees or shrubs should be noted, along with features such as paving and paths and the material the boundaries are made from. Next, take the tape and fix it to one boundary close to the house. Run it across the rear of the building and parallel to it, all the way to the other side. Leave the tape in place and check the consecutive distances of all the features that you marked. The corner of the house might be about 3ft. (1m), one side of the French doors at 5ft. 3in. (1.6m), the other side at 6ft. 6in. (2m) and so on until you get to the other side. Once this set of measurements is complete, run the tape the other way, at 90 degrees to the first, down the garden and check all the relevant measurements in that direction.

LONG NARROW YARD

This narrow yard (right) has a length-to-width ratio of about one to five. Given the shape of the yard, one would normally think of using a rectangular pattern to link it strongly with the building, but here a circular terrace is particularly successful, the sweep of brick being echoed by the raised beds and curved steps. A path then sweeps away under the pergola and crosses the lawn before pivoting past an apple tree to terminate at the informal brick-paved sitting area that fronts a summer house. Beyond this, a gate leads through a high wall to the secret garden. Its hidden location makes use of surprise, one of the most important elements in good backyard design.

KEY: 1 Gate; 2 Tree; 3 Secret Garden; 4 Mixed Planting; 5 Brick Paving; 6 Summer House; 7 Pergola; 8 Millstone; 9 Raised Bed; 10 Steps.

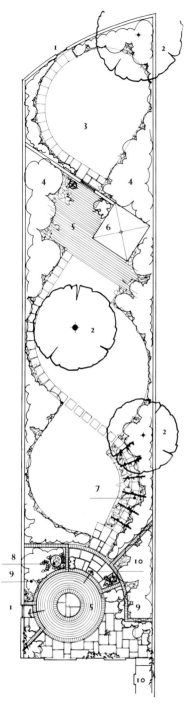

**PLAN FOR A
LONG NARROW YARD**

CHANGES IN LEVEL

Once the main linear measurements are complete, check any changes of level. The height of steps and retaining walls is easy enough to note by using a short steel tape measure. Sloping lawns are slightly more difficult, but can be checked by sighting back towards the house so that your eye is level with a particular point and then measuring the distance to the ground.

PREVAILING WINDS

A chill wind can prevent us from enjoying the yard, and for much of the year this will come from a particular "prevailing" direction. If wind is a problem, check the prevailing direction and mark it on your survey so that you can provide an effective windbreak.

GOOD OR BAD VIEWS

We are so often preoccupied with what goes on within our plot that we tend to forget that there is a world outside. Good views are a bonus and should be left open or even emphasized. Bad views—an overlooking upstairs window or the back of a neighbor's garage—should be screened, either with a solid structure of some kind or by planting.

SOIL

The type of soil in your garden or yard will largely determine what you can grow. Acid soil is at one end of the spectrum and alkaline at the other; plants happy in one type may be quite the opposite in the other. A soil midway between the two is neutral and will allow you to grow a wide range of species. Buy a simple soil-testing kit from any garden center and take samples from various parts of the plot. Most kits provide lists of plants that will thrive in any given soil type.

ANGLE

I have left the most important piece of survey information to last. This involves checking the way the yard faces in relation to the passage of the sun. Checking this is where that compass comes in handy, so you can easily verify the position of north and south. Remember that the sun rises in the east and sets in the west and that in winter it will be a good deal lower and cast longer shadows than in the summer.

Far left: *Courtyards can make fine sheltered gardens which have the benefit of direct access from the house on a number of sides. An architectural design like this one is often the best choice. Setts that could have been part of the old floor make ideal paving, while the solid roof-supports act as host to scrambling climbers that frame the shady porch.*

Left: *Roof gardens are in a world of their own and, while the views may be superb, the growing conditions can be harsh. Shelter is often vital and this lattice screen is perfect for both plants and people, picking up the pattern of the wrought-iron furniture.*

SQUARE YARD

Square yards are the most difficult of all to design as they are absolutely static. There are two basic ways to handle the problem: either use a circular pattern that will disguise the shape or use a series of interlocking rectangles that build upon the basic outline and create far greater interest from it. This is precisely what I have done in this tiny town garden (left) with a collage of water, paving, and planting. Some of the beds are raised to give young planting a boost and to soften the walls, while the overhead beams cast light shade on the sitting area below. The seat and barbecue are built-in to save space in such a limited area, and pots of plants, ideal on a terrace or patio, provide instant color.

PLAN FOR A SQUARE YARD

KEY: 1 Raised Bed; 2 Overhead Beams and Climbers; 3 Built-in Seating; 4 Seat; 5 Slatted Fence; 6 York Stone; 7 Brick Paving; 8 Barbecue; 9 Pond; 10 Tree; 11 Mixed Planting; 12 Pots.

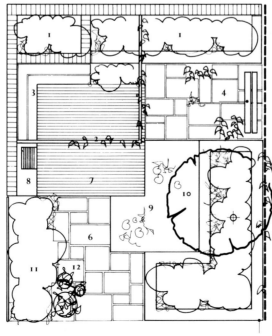

5

Right: *Dividing a yard into separate rooms or areas is an important aspect of garden design. The white bench here nestles into a niche in the hedges, but the eye is drawn into another space by the carefully positioned tree and topiary. The hedges have also been clipped at different heights, with rounded contours that are altogether softer and more comfortable than a crisp rectangular outline. This composition is all about symmetry: the vertical line and size of the tree act as a counter-balance to the longer and lower line of the hedge below, while the seat acts as a punctuation mark to "lift" the quiet background.*

Far right: *Why do people always paint picket fences white? White paint can often glare and is a chore to maintain. With a spectrum of color available, think positive and go for something like this striking blue. You could use the color somewhere else in the yard—on the weatherboarding of the house or on a well-painted building.*

THE DESIGN

Now that the survey is complete, you can start to think about the actual design and just what you want to see in the finished yard. This really is a family job: after all, the finished composition is going to have to cater for everyone and everything. Start to make a list, jotting down every requirement you and other members of your family can think of. In a typical backyard this might include a patio for sitting and dining, a barbecue, raised beds, a pool, a lawn and a play area, as well as a shed, a greenhouse, somewhere to put the bikes, and an arbor or area of built-in seating. Remember, too, that a yard has to contain the ugly as well as the practical, so the dustbins, washing line, compost heap and incinerator will have to fit somewhere!

If the list seems endless, don't worry—you can always thin it down later. It is more important that you leave nothing out, as it's much more difficult to incorporate a major feature once the design is complete.

PREPARING A DRAWING

Making a scaled drawing from your survey is straightforward. You will need to use a sheet of graph paper, selecting one or a number of squares to represent a foot or meter on the ground. Starting with the house, transfer all your measurements onto the graph paper, including the position of doors and windows, drains, slopes, and everything else you noted down. Mark the direction of the prevailing wind if there was one, any good or bad views, the length of the shadows, and so on. Pretty soon you will have a survey drawing, which will provide the basis for the finished design. Make several photocopies and file the original drawing for safe-keeping.

To prepare the final design drawing, tape a copy of the survey onto a clean surface and place a sheet of tracing paper over it. At first, just rough in the broad position of features. The area allocated for a patio might logically be at the rear of the house if it is in full sun, but if shade is a problem it may be some distance away, served by a sensible path. A barbecue would ideally be close to the kitchen, a pond in full view of the main windows of the house, while the shed, greenhouse, and utility areas should be grouped together, and screened in some way. If your plans include an arbor, this could be built in a quiet corner. Work in pencil and have an eraser handy to rub out any mistakes. You can also sketch in alternatives before making a final choice; there are bound to be plenty of changes initially!

At this stage, just allocate space so that the yard starts to work in overall terms. You needn't worry about exact dimensions of a feature or the pattern and material for the paving until later.

HARD LANDSCAPING

Once you are happy with the approximate position and the size of each feature, you can fill in the detail by firming the design up and finalizing the list of features you want to incorporate. It's worth bearing in mind that the "hard landscape" areas of paving and walling will take the lion's share of any budget. Plan these to link sensibly with the adjoining house. If the building is of brick, then brick might also be used in part of the patio or to build raised beds; if the floors inside the building are stone then this could be run outside to form a patio that will link the two elements together.

As has already been emphasized, simplicity is so often the key to success. By keeping the materials used for hard surfaces to a minimum, you are far more likely to achieve a harmonious result. Of course, a large expanse of yard covered in a single material may look visually heavy—especially if you are using new bricks or concrete flagstones—and in such instances it can be a positive benefit to mix materials: a brick path flanked by stone setts or railroad ties, or a checkboard pattern of flagstones and cobbles. Never underestimate, either, the softening effects of sympathetic planting: shrubs spilling over on to a path, or grass and moss growing in the cracks between bricks or flagstones can mellow even the most recently landscaped plot, integrating your hard surfaces with the other features of your yard to create a living outdoor room.

More "fluid" surfacing materials include gravel, cobbles, and even tarmac. These can be laid to a flowing pattern, and are ideal for a sweeping driveway or a meandering path, where granite setts or flagstones would need to be cut to fit. They can also demand less on the eye than other, larger-module materials, something to be borne in mind, particularly in smaller yards.

If you look at the designs in this chapter you will also see that the layout close to the house is planned in an "architectural" and positive way, helping to draw house and yard together as a single entity. Further away you can start to think in more fluid terms, planning the shape of lawns and borders in strong flowing curves. These provide a real feeling of room and movement, which in turn creates an impression of greater space, even in a compact garden.

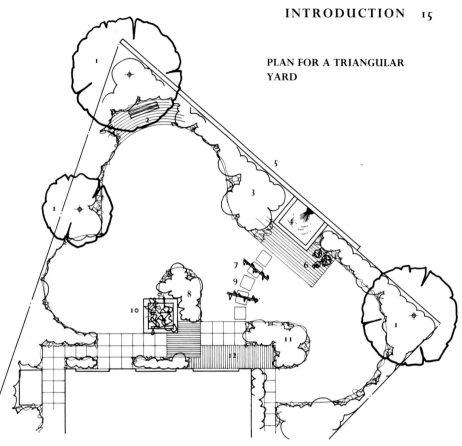

PLAN FOR A TRIANGULAR YARD

PLANTING

While the planting scheme is beyond the scope of this book, it is, of course, the essential element that brings any yard or garden to life, the plants embracing your composition so that they clothe and soften the inevitably hard lines of paving and walling. I think I have already made it clear that trying to create a yard without planning it first will almost certainly lead to disaster. This is particularly true of planting. At all costs, avoid over-complicated planting schemes. Do your homework, check a good plant directory, and go about this all-important planning in a logical sequence—it will pay enormous dividends in the long run. Think first about where you might position trees, bearing in mind their size and their ability to provide shade or a screen. Next plan your shrubs: fast-growing evergreens will quickly provide shelter and protection. Finally, fill in the details and add color with a selection of bulbs and herbaceous perennials, and set aside areas for annuals and containers for a change of planting from year to year.

TRIANGULAR YARD

Triangular yards are always awkward as they tend to focus the view in a particular direction. In this design I have demonstrated the principle of providing an architectural pattern close to the building. The brick paving leads out from the French windows and interlocks with the raised bed and planting to form an attractive combination of hard and soft landscape. From here the eye is led away at an angle, under the pergola and towards the raised pool.

The apex of the triangle is naturally dominant and virtually impossible to hide. It is best not to bother; soften it by all means with well-chosen plants, but allow the eye to rest there with a purpose. The seat, placed alongside a tree at the end of this garden, has the added bonus of an attractive view back across the yard.

KEY: 1 Tree; 2 Seat on Brick Paving; 3 Mixed Planting; 4 Raised Pool and Spout; 5 Wall; 6 Pots; 7 Pergola; 8 Herbs; 9 Stepping Stones; 10 Raised Bed for Annuals; 11 Roses; 12 Brick Paving.

Opposite: *Water is a delightful influence in any yard, but needs to match the mood of the overall design. In this situation, the informal pool echoes the sweep of lawn that is in turn softened by planting. While a calm surface sets up reflections, a little movement adds enormous interest. The flume in the foreground is designed to allow a trickle of water to overflow the bowl and drop into the pool below. A dovecot provides a more distant focal point against trees and shrubs.*

Above left: *This window through a wall focuses the view beyond to glorious effect. A glimpse provides that vital element of mystery as well as creating a feeling of tension before you enter the next "room".*

PATHS
AND PATIOS

*Paths and patios are the hard landscape "bones" of your yard
and provide the design framework around which the
softer elements of lawns, planting and other features can be
positioned. They are crucial to your enjoyment of the
yard, providing areas for sitting, dining, play and many other
activities as well as access to other features.
Simplicity and strength of purpose are all-important in this part
of the design. You should choose your materials carefully
from the vast range available, taking your time over the choice
and thinking about the visual and cost implications.
Paving is perhaps the most long-term investment in your
yard; make sure it is right for you and your situation before
you buy. Any paving close to the house will relate
strongly to it, so this should also influence your choice. Look
around your area to see what materials predominate
locally, and use them for the most sympathetic result.*

*All the materials used here are
natural rather than man-made,
which allows them to relate to
one another. The gravel path
provides a purpose for the old
wire pergola and the paving gives
a place to sit, while the planting
draws the composition together.
The bowls, piled high with flints,
provide a humorous counterpoint.*

Left: This path is built from granite setts, with a step constructed from the same material. Planting softens the outline to either side, and moss has been allowed to grow up in the gaps between the setts. The stone spheres provide attractive and unusual punctuation.

Opposite: Gravel is an ideal surface for a circular patio as it will take up any shape. This design is built up from a series of circles that include the outer ring of planting, the brick-edged pool, the terracotta pots, and even the stone orbs. The gentle curves naturally incline the eye to the pond, which acts as a focal point. Only the sundial and the seat disrupt the pattern.

Apart from the aesthetics of choosing the right material for a patio or path, you will also need to allocate enough space, particularly for a patio. If you think of your yard as an outside room, or series of rooms, then the main paved terrace will take up a similar proportion of the available area to, say, your sitting-room inside the house. An absolute minimum size would be 12 × 12ft. (3.6 × 3.6m) which provides enough space for four people to sit around a table. If you can make it more generous, then do so: far better to be able to push a chair back with plenty of room to spare than risk tipping over into the nearest flower bed with a drink in your hand!

The overall shape of the paving will be important too. This is often the first point of entry into the yard, especially at the front of the house and is likely to set the theme for the entire composition. There may be scope here for raised beds, and in the back garden for built-in seating and a barbecue. Overhead beams can provide light shade and are invaluable in screening you from an adjacent window. Train a climber over them to soften the line and provide fragrance for the area below. If high walls flank your patio, they can also support climbers or may be used to extend a color scheme from the inside out. This is

particularly effective in a town yard linked to the house by floor-to-ceiling windows or sliding patio doors. Water is another option, ranging from the formality of a rectangular pool, complete with fountain, to a simple millstone, set within an area of loose cobbles and planting, with water sliding over the surface from a tank concealed below.

While patios concentrate activity in a given area, paths are built for access, both around the house and through the yard. The smoother the surface, the quicker the action: a crisp surface of precast slabs encourages speed, while a path laid with irregular cobbles slows you down, both visually and physically. Very often the material chosen for the patio will be suitable for the paths too, providing continuity. But whatever you use, do make sure the path is wide enough, remembering that it may well have planting to either side that will spill over and soften the outline, reducing the width to some extent.

Whatever your final choice, remember that the materials for a patio or path will last a lifetime. They form the basic framework of your yard, and can only be changed with difficulty and at great expense, in terms of time, money and inconvenience. Planning is therefore vital.

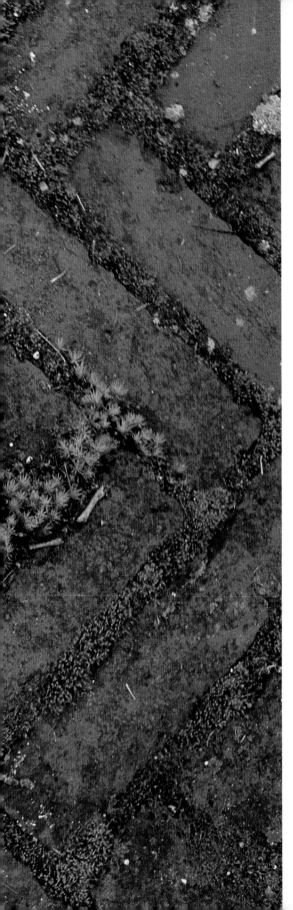

BRICK

Brick paving is extremely versatile. If your house is also built of brick, you can use it in the backyard to create strong visual links between the two areas. It can be teamed with another surface if used as panels or contrasting courses, or laid alone to make a superb path or patio. Because a brick is a small module it can be laid to a curving or circular pattern without cutting, making it particularly suitable for the sweeping line of a path or for a strongly shaped patio.

Before buying bricks you should always check the density. A rough meaure of this can be made by twisting a coin on the surface as hard as possible. If no damage is apparent then the surface will be pretty resistant. Not all bricks are suitable for paving. Only the harder types will withstand the pressures of feet and frost. Up until a few years ago the choice was between house-facing bricks or very hard and shiny "engineering" bricks. While these can still be used—and engineering bricks look very good in a crisp "architectural" situation—purpose-made brick "paviors" that are about half the thickness of a standard house brick are now produced in a variety of styles.

Brick paving should be laid over a sub-base of well-compacted hardcore and either bedded on a semi-dry mortar mix, with dry mortar brushed into the joints, or on a wet mortar mix, with careful pointing of the joints to avoid any staining of the surface. Another method uses bricks butted together, without mortar, over a layer of hardcore. The edges of a path or patio must be firmly set in concrete to prevent movement of the overall surface.

A number of different "bonds" (patterns) can be used, each of which has a different visual emphasis. Stretcher bond along a path tends to accelerate a view, but if laid in the opposite direction, across the path, it slows the eye down. Herringbone is a complicated and relatively "busy" pattern, while basketweave bond is altogether more static.

Because of their textured surface, bricks soon mellow and can be quickly colonized by mosses and lichens. This makes them ideal in a traditional design or a cottage garden where the patina of age looks just right.

Herringbone is a visually complicated but fascinating pattern that is often used in a traditional design situation. Here the surface is delightfully covered with mosses and lichens, adding to the feeling of age and maturity.

Opposite above left: This crisply designed path is made of bricks butted together in a basketweave pattern without mortar joints. The soldier-course edging is softened by overhanging plants.

Opposite above right: This path illustrates the way that bricks can be laid to a curving pattern. Stretcher bond leads the eye on to the timber bridge, although the step here is perhaps too shallow, making a trip likely.

Opposite below left: These old bricks look just right laid dry in a basketweave pattern. The unpointed, irregular bonds offer the chance to introduce low-growing plants such as thyme. The planting ensures that this is a path for a stroll rather than a brisk walk, while the perfectly positioned copper pot provides a pleasing focal point.

Opposite below right: A brick floor is ideal for use in courtyard gardens. This carefully laid herringbone-pattern patio provides plenty of room for sitting and entertaining. The plant-filled terracotta pots add a pretty splash of color, while the lush surrounding foliage softens the walls.

Right: *A gravel path is attractive, practical and associates particularly well with planting. And the crunch of gravel underfoot has a particular charisma all its own. This path is neatly edged with boards and passes beneath a well-detailed pergola.*

Below: *This Japanese-style path simulates the bed of a stream, with rocks and boulders breaking the flow. The thin, sculptural leaves of iris are the perfect foil to the water-washed stones.*

GRAVEL

Gravel is a versatile, attractive and relatively cheap paving material. It can look equally at home as the base for a patio in a formal town yard or as a sweeping drive in the country, but correct laying is essential if you are to avoid an uncomfortable "treadmill" effect when trying to cross your path or patio.

Always ensure that gravel is laid on a solid sub-base of well-compacted hardcore, the thickness of which should be between 3in. (7cm) and 6in. (15cm), depending on the underlying soil type and the amount of traffic—either cars or pedestrians. Over the hardcore lay a 2in. (5cm) layer of 2in. (5cm) diameter gravel and roll this in well. The next layer will be a 2in. (5cm) layer of fine gravel, mixed with hoggin—a clay mixture available from the same gravel pit. This will act as a binder to the final layer of $\frac{3}{8}$in. (1cm) diameter washed pea gravel that should be top-dressed over the surface and rolled in well. To ensure the final finish is well compacted and firm underfoot, a heavy roller should be used over the surface at all stages of the job.

Unlike paving, gravel is a "fluid" surface and often needs retaining at the edges. One option is to use long timber boards or railroad ties, treated with non-toxic preservative and pegged in position with stakes. A more handsome, and more expensive, alternative would be to use bricks set in concrete. Precast concrete kerb edging should be avoided, particularly if curved borders are required.

Where gravel adjoins planting, it can be simply run under the latter without a defining edge so that the two surfaces overlap one another. Plants can also be spot-planted within an area of gravel and broad foliage acts as an excellent foil to the much smaller stones. If, however, you use gravel next to grass, you should ensure the grass is set at least 4in. (10cm) above the gravel surface and is retained at the edges. This will prevent stones from being caught in mower blades when you cut the grass. Maintenance is generally low, although fallen leaves can be a nuisance, requiring regular raking in the autumn.

Gravel is available in a wide variety of colors, depending on its area of origin. Pale gravel has a great ability to reflect light, and you can use this

to good advantage in shady areas or basement gardens. White chippings will transform a gloomy corner, looking particularly effective when teamed with another contrasting surface such as slate. Another point in gravel's favor is its use as a burglar deterrent or guest early-warning system, since it's impossible to approach a house along a gravel path or drive without immediately alerting the residents. However, parents of small children may have less positive feelings about gravel. There is no doubt that children find it hard on the knees when they fall, and they do tend to enjoy "sowing" it all over the lawn, giving their parents the less enjoyable task of sweeping it off again. There is also the danger that children will put the gravel in their mouths, which is unhygienic and could be dangerous.

CHIPPINGS

While gravel is normally rounded; stone chippings are usually angular. Smaller than cobbles, chippings, like gravel, come in a variety of colors. Often the main hard surfacing material in formal Japanese gardens, chippings can be used to dramatic effect. In a basement town garden, a hard surface area covered in white chippings (obtained from calcinated flint stone) will help to maximize the available light, reflecting it and "opening up" the space. And plants with dark green foliage look particularly striking growing alongside white chippings. Wood and bark chippings, although more commonly used as a ground mulch to help prevent weeds, can look effective as surfaces for pathways in rural environments and lend yards an organic feel.

The different textures of gravels, glass marbles and ceramics are contrasted in this delightful plot designed by Hilary McMahon. Broad steps drop down to a pool, with a gravel beach that is in turn flanked by planting. The maintenance requirements of this set-up are extremely low.

STONE

NATURAL STONE

This is the most expensive and finest paving available. It can be found in a vast range of types, colors, shapes and textures, looking superb in any well-designed yard.

As with all surfaces, it should be used within the overall context of the setting. While fine, old, second-hand sandstone flags would naturally look out of place adjoining a high-tech steel-and-glass facade, the same stone would look superb laid as a terrace in a more traditional situation. Random rectangular slabs of stone of uneven thickness are often available, and can be laid on carefully levelled and compacted ground with a bed of sifted soil or sand. This type of paving need not necessarily be pointed, and joints can be left open to allow colonization by low, ground-hugging plants. You should work out a paving pattern from a central "key" stone and try to ensure that the joints between the slabs are staggered. Small spaces can be left empty to form planting pockets or filled with brick to relieve the appearance.

SLATE

In contrast to natural stone, slate has a naturally sleek, architectural appearance and often looks better wet than dry. Its dark color ideally suits it to a sunny situation, where it can either form an entire terrace or path, or be used in strips or squares to contrast with another kind of paving.

GRANITE

Every bit as hard as it looks, granite is often hewn into brick-sized full setts or smaller half setts. The surface is slightly uneven, so it is not always ideal for a patio where tables and chairs are present, but setts are ideal for a path or drive, where the surface offers greater grip than a smooth paving.

MARBLE

The exorbitant cost of marble is usually enough to deter most people from using it to lay a patio. It is undeniably exotic and, while it looks great in an Italian piazza, it looks appalling used as crazy paving in a suburban backyard. Just occasionally it fits into a highly controlled pattern adjoining a contemporary building, but it should usually be avoided.

Granite setts are easily laid to a pattern. This fan shape is both traditional and attractive. The somewhat harsh color is tempered by grass, while the irregularity of the stones emphasizes the natural character of the material.

Opposite above left: *Stepping stones draw both the eye and foot across a lawn or planted area. This path meanders towards a distant arch and disappears, with a slight air of mystery, before finally reaching the house.*

Opposite above right: *These slate slabs are butted tightly together, at an angle to the surrounding bricks, to form a perfectly smooth and sophisticated patio. The planting has been particularly well chosen and positioned to temper the crisp composition.*

Opposite below: *Solid riven slabs of stone form a stepping-stone path through a bed of loose cobbles. Simple timber boards contain the cobbles, while a predominantly green planting scheme provides a quiet background.*

WOOD

Wood is ideal for many projects in the garden, and is particularly useful for decking and steps. Like a stone patio adjacent to a stone house, a wooden deck adjoining a wooden building will make a strong link between inside and outside. Wood can be easily worked to shapes that would be extremely difficult to produce using paving. It is light, it warms up quickly and it needs little maintenance apart from a regular application of non-toxic preservative. Never use creosote, which is certain death to plants. Some wood can even be bought already pressure-treated with preservative, further reducing after-care. Remember, though, that wood means trees, and if those trees come from a non-managed source then you are contributing to the degradation of our environment. Please check with your supplier, particularly if you envisage using hardwood species from tropical rain forests.

The sturdy and heavy bulk of railroad ties makes them ideal for paving, raised beds and retaining walls. Try and select your ties before you buy, as they may be soaked with oil or tar which will cause you problems in hot weather. Because of their weight, it really is a two-man job to lift them, but they are solid enough to be bedded on a minimal foundation of sifted soil over well-compacted ground or they can be laid in a staggered bond like brickwork. Raised beds are fast to build, and again the ties can be laid like bricks, their weight allowing them to be laid dry. However, if you are constructing a retaining wall, or a raised bed that is more than three tiers high, the ties should be drilled to accept vertical steel rods that are then bedded into a concrete foundation to ensure stability.

If your yard includes a change in level, ties can make excellent steps. Rather than making a straight flight, you might prefer a staggered pattern with planting encroaching on either side. Steps can also be built from logs securely pegged into the slope. In a steep flight they should be bedded close together, but with a more gentle gradient, the treads can be floored with chipped bark.

Raised beds or retaining walls can be built from sawn logs arranged vertically to follow any

line, straight or curved. Assuming the logs will rise about 24in. (600mm) above ground, you should bury them 12in. (300mm) below ground for stability, first soaking them thoroughly in a non-toxic preservative.

Large logs can be sliced up into discs about 6in. (15cm) thick and used as stepping stones. More unusually, they could even be made to form a kind of patio. If they become slippery, chicken wire nailed over each slice will solve the problem and be virtually invisible.

Above: *Logs set into a slope and firmly pegged in place make a delightfully informal flight of steps. Such a feature invites you to explore the garden and creates a practical and interesting focal point. Here the treads are left simply as rougher grass with planting softening the edges, but chipped bark or gravel could be used instead.*

Opposite: *Wood has been used at all levels in this garden. The deck is built from neatly squared boards and the theme is continued in the well-detailed raised beds. At the highest level the overhead beams would provide excellent supports for climbing plants and will cast light shade, extending the line of the patio out into the surrounding planting.*

SUN DECK

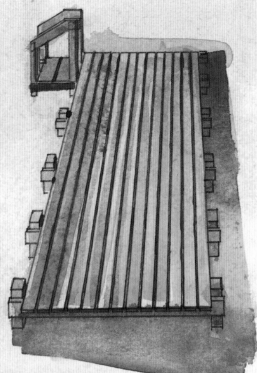

This deck measures about 12ft. (3.6m) square and provides an informal seating area some distance from the house and close to the pool. The lumber has been carefully "distressed" to expose the grain. This was achieved by lightly burning the surface of the wood with a blow torch and then using a wire brush to remove softer wood, leaving the tougher grain slightly raised.

CONSTRUCTION

Mark the area to be covered by the deck and remove any turf. Next, excavate to a depth of 4–6in. (100–150mm), then backfill the area with crushed stone or gravel. Make sure it is well compacted and that the surface is level.

The height of the deck should be 6–12in. (150–300mm). The deck shown here is supported on beams that run between 4 × 4in. (100 × 100mm) posts protruding 12in. (300mm) above the ground. Cut the posts to length: you will need to sink them about 18in. (450mm) into the ground, and then allow for the 12in. (300mm) height plus an additional 2in. (50mm) that projects above the supporting beams. Soak all the wood in a nontoxic, exterior-grade wood preservative and leave to dry.

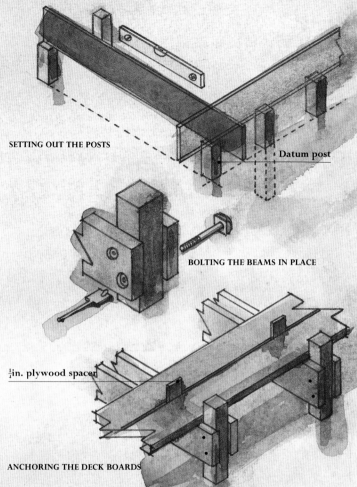

SETTING OUT THE POSTS

Datum post

BOLTING THE BEAMS IN PLACE

$\frac{1}{4}$in. plywood spacer

ANCHORING THE DECK BOARDS

Calculate the positions of the second row of posts by using one of the 2 × 6in. (50 × 150mm) beams marked with the post spacings as a guide. Set up a line at right angles to the datum post and accurately set the corner post. Check that the post is vertical and the top level with the datum post by using a level and straightedge from the opposite post on the first side. Repeat for the remaining posts, checking each one and securing it in place.

Using C-clamps, clamp a beam along the inside of one pair of posts, 2in. (50mm) down from the top of the posts plus the thickness of the deck boards. Mark the top and bottom of the beam on all posts and extend these lines to the sides using a square. Mark bolt hole positions on the posts diagonally within the rectangles and drill clearance holes just large enough for the bolts.

Clamp a beam between two posts so that it extends 2in. (50mm) over each end. Use the post clearance holes as a guide to drill through the

beam. Repeat for another beam on the opposite side of the posts. Counterbore one beam to accept the nuts, then bolt both to the posts using 8in. (200mm) long $\frac{1}{2}$in. (M12) bolts. Repeat for all beams.

You can now start to fit the deck itself. Position the first board $\frac{1}{4}$in. (6mm) clear of the line of posts by using plywood spacers and screw down into the center line of each beam. Use the plywood spacers to position the second board and screw in place. Continue the operation, one board at a time, across the deck.

To build a step leading to the deck, set three posts outside the deck floor, but opposite and parallel to three main posts. Bolt 2 × 3in. (50 × 75mm) bearers between them and the corresponding main deck posts, directly beneath the beams. The central post is cut short to fit under a step at deck level. Cut the outer posts about 36in. (900mm) longer for the handrail, which is recessed to the inside faces. Glue and screw in place.

Bore or dig a hole 22in. (550mm) deep using a post-hole borer or a shovel. Fill the bottom of the hole with 4in. (100mm) of well-packed gravel and set the post top at a level 2in. (50mm) above the proposed deck surface. This will be the "datum" post, from which all the other posts are set out and checked against. Check the post vertically in both directions using a level and then ram soil around the post or set it in concrete to hold it in place. If you use concrete, bring the mix very slightly higher than ground level and round it over so that water runs away from the post. Leave the concrete to dry.

Mark out the remaining five post positions down one of the deck at 27in. (680mm) centers. Bore the remaining holes and position the posts as described above. Make sure that the tops of all the posts are level: use a straightedge and level to check this, always working from the datum post.

Now work out the distance to the opposite side. It is best to use a random arrangement of 1 × 6in. (25 × 150mm) and 1 × 7in. (25 × 175mm) boards which have been planed down by about $\frac{1}{4}$in. (6mm). Allow a $\frac{1}{4}$in. (6mm) gap between each board for drainage.

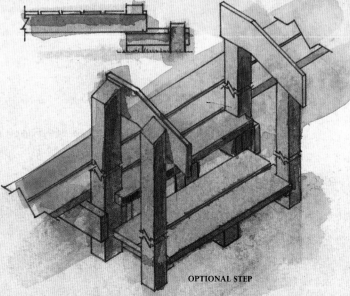

OPTIONAL STEP

Above: *Where space is limited, the only option is to build upwards. This is a pedestal for pots on a three-tier wooden platform. Plant color is mainly restricted to grays and pinks, teaming perfectly with the soft tones of terracotta.*

Right: *Breakfast on a warm patio is a pleasure no one should deny themselves, but remember that furnishings should blend well with their environment. These wickerwork seats have been chosen to echo the warm color of the stone sets.*

Opposite above: *This roof garden is floored with lightweight tiles and surrounded by raised beds. White-painted screens help to filter the wind, while the pots are safely positioned away from the parapet walls.*

Opposite below: *Pots of plants will soften the flat expanse of a large patio, providing instant color throughout the year. Here, the uniform color of the terracotta pots provides visual continuity.*

PATIOS

A patio is very often the hub of activity around which the rest of the yard revolves. In some cases, such as a courtyard or tiny town yard, it can take up almost the entire area available, with planting softening the edges of the plot. In a larger composition it may share the space with sweeping lawns, borders, raised beds, vegetable gardens, and a range of other features.

As well as providing a site for sitting and dining, most patios have to cater for children's play, household chores and the repair of anything from bikes to car engines. We have already seen that you need ample space and have looked at the wide range of materials available for construction. If in doubt, and you can afford it, always make the patio larger than you initially think; it will be well worth it later on.

Of course the area may not always be at ground level: roof gardens are immensely attractive, even though they do pose all kinds of problems in constructional and horticultural terms. It is exciting to create an outside room in this Mary Poppins world of wide skies and chimney pots, but always check that the roof is strong enough to take the additional weight required. If in doubt, call on the services of a qualified architect or surveyor. His or her fee will be more than worth it if you are then able to rest easy at night without the horrific prospect of a ton of soggy compost arriving unexpectedly on your bed! Other aspects of safety are also important: a pot knocked over at ground level is no problem, but the same container falling from a roof could be very dangerous indeed.

Because a patio is essentially a hard landscape feature it will benefit enormously from the provision of planting. As a general rule plants grow far better in the ground than in pots. So, although pots are invaluable for instant color throughout the year, you should try to leave some areas in and around your patio open for plants. Raised beds are both practical and attractive options for the patio: you can vary the soil in them to suit a particular type of planting, you can use their sides as occasional seating, and if you wish to provide an area for children, you can convert them to sandpits or other play areas which can later revert to their original purpose.

Above: *Dining in such a pretty gazebo is definitely up-market, but nevertheless delightful. On a practical note, the roof provides shelter in case of rain.*

Above right: *Tea on the terrace is a perfect way to spend a summer afternoon. Wicker furniture always looks good and is light enough to move around easily. Gravel provides a sensible floor, allowing planting to grow through the surface.*

Right: *Some barbecues are gas-fired, either from a bottle stored below or from a piped mains supply. This one is of ample size, with plenty of room on the terrace to allow unhindered cooking; planting at the side would greatly soften the impact and blend the barbecue into the overall composition.*

Opposite above: *This outside room has been as carefully designed as any within the house. The circular pattern of setts has been beautifully laid in concentric courses, the round table sitting right in the middle. The table cloth and chair covers match this pattern, while following the pink, blue and mauve colors of the attractive planting scheme.*

Opposite below: *Who said romance was dead? What could be more charming than sitting in this idyllic setting beneath the trees, sharing dinner? The rest of the yard and world are incidental, it's the moment that counts.*

OUTDOOR EATING

One of the best reasons for having a patio of ample size is that it allows you to take meals outside. To do this comfortably you need a dining area that is well sheltered, both from cold winds and any overlooking windows that threaten privacy. Because paving and walling are likely to predominate, planting will be essential. It is worth remembering that this often provides a much more effective filter for the wind than a solid fence or screen.

Fragrance is another benefit of carefully chosen planting in this area, especially if you train climbers along overhead beams. There is nothing more delightful than sitting outside surrounded by such plants as honeysuckle, jasmine or roses. Many species are at their most scented in the evening, at just the time when you are likely to use the patio most.

Subtle lighting is essential if you are going to get the best out of your outside room. As well as the straightforward illumination of an area in practical terms, you have the option of highlighting a particular feature or focal point. But, as with any aspect of design, keep things as simple as possible. There are some ghastly fittings available that are not only pretentious but downright ugly. Remember that it is the light that is important, not the fitting. The location of a beam or soft glow is also important: there is little point in illuminating the top of your head, but a fitting positioned at working height beside a barbecue or at ground level close to steps can be practical as well as attractive.

Lighting requires electricity, and one option is to install a completely waterproof ring main around your garden. This can be used to power various tools and features, but you should always bear safety in mind, and it is strongly recommended that you take professional advice and enroll the services of a fully qualified electrician if in any doubt whatsoever.

Finally, don't forget that we're not the only creatures to eat outside—birds, mammals and a multitude of insects live out there too. A bird table or bath is an essential garden feature, and if you can avoid the use of pesticides and sprays then make every effort to do so, as it will benefit the flora and fauna.

BARBECUE

Eating outside is one of the great pleasures in life. If you like barbecuing—and millions do—then you should go about it in a positive way. Small readymade barbecues can rarely cook enough for a big gathering of ravenous friends: what you need is a large, well-built one of the kind shown here.

It is easy to plan such a feature in the initial stages of building a patio, but, if you are careful, you could incorporate it into an existing layout, as long as solid foundations are dug.

Protect your patio while building is in progress by covering the surrounding surface with heavy-gauge plastic and lapping the edges of the sheets into the excavation. Then weigh them down.

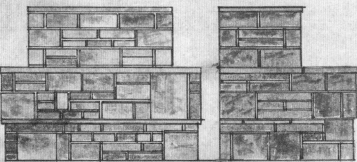

BACK ELEVATION   SIDE ELEVATION

FRONT ELEVATION

CONSTRUCTION

Excavate an 8in. (200mm) deep rectangular base measuring 6ft. 6in. × 4ft. 6in. (2 × 1.5m). Spread an even layer of gravel in the bottom of the excavation and compact this to a finished thickness of 4in. (100mm). Spread sand across the surface to fill in any gaps. Cover the gravel with 4in. (100mm) of concrete and level it *off flush with the surrounding surface using a straight-edged board. You should then leave the concrete to dry for about a week; to make sure that it dries evenly, keep it covered with damp sacks if the weather is hot, and with plastic sheeting of some kind if there is a chance of frost.*

Plan the stonework in advance by laying the pattern out on the ground. The barbecue shown here has a worktop height of about 31in. (800mm) and a height to the top of the flue of 51in. (1295mm). Avoid vertical joints that coincide with one another in succeeding courses (layers). At the corners, blocks should be bonded together so that they overlap and provide greater strength. You can draw the plan and elevations out on tracing paper, but make several copies as some will be bound to get dirty or lost! The sizes we have used are: $2\frac{1}{2} \times 7\frac{1}{2}$in. $(65 \times 190mm)$; $2\frac{1}{2} \times 8\frac{1}{2}$in. $(65 \times 215mm)$; $2\frac{1}{2} \times 11\frac{1}{2}$in. $(65 \times 290mm)$; $5\frac{1}{2} \times 11\frac{1}{2}$in. $(137 \times 290mm)$; $8\frac{1}{2} \times 11\frac{1}{2}$in. $(215 \times 290mm)$; and $2\frac{1}{2} \times 17\frac{1}{2}$in. $(65 \times 445mm)$, all 4in. (100mm) thick. The barbecue also needs 2in. (50mm) thick copings measuring $10\frac{1}{4} \times 24$in. $(260 \times 610mm)$ and 5×24in. $(125 \times 610mm)$, and 24×24in. $(610 \times 610mm)$ paving slabs.

First construct the four supporting walls to a height of 9in (225mm).

Bed the slabs beneath the charcoal tray between the two center supporting walls; one course higher, bed the floor slabs for the log storage on the right-hand side. Lay a course of coping on top of the slabs, then build up the center walls, inserting $\frac{1}{4} \times 4$in. (6 × 100mm) mild steel strips, 48in. (1220mm) long, to support the charcoal tray and the cooking grid as indicated. Bed angled copings above the fifth course of bricks. Build up the front, back and two end walls to the height of the center supporting walls, incorporating a coping course at the back to maintain the correct bonding. Openings in the back wall provide additional storage space.

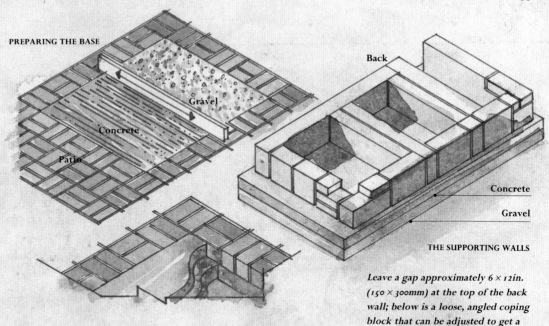

PREPARING THE BASE

Gravel

Concrete

Patio

Back

Concrete

Gravel

THE SUPPORTING WALLS

Two paving slabs are used on each side to form the worktops. The flue arch is supported by a semicircular "turning piece" with an internal radius of $11\frac{1}{2}$in. (290mm). It is made from a 48in. (1220mm) length of $\frac{1}{4} \times 4$in. (6 × 100mm) mild steel strip bent into shape: the ends should be bent at right angles to form 4in. (100mm) projections. Make a plywood template and take it to a blacksmith or steel fabricator who can make the turning piece for you.

Bed the turning piece in mortar. Build up the blocks for the flue section around the arch, one course at a time. A number of blocks will need to be cut to fit around the arch. Carefully score all around the block where you want the break to be. Bed the block in sand, then give one or two sharp blows with a hammer and chisel to sever the block. Careful pointing around the break will make up any discrepancies in the cutting.

Leave a gap approximately 6 × 12in. (150 × 300mm) at the top of the back wall; below is a loose, angled coping block that can be adjusted to get a good draft in the flue. Finally, cap the flue with one or more continuous lengths of slab.

FLUE DETAIL

Top

Back

Flue

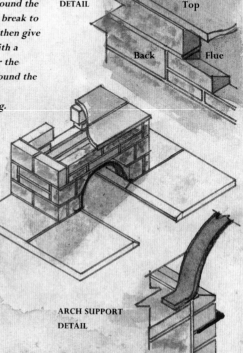

FORMING THE WORKTOPS

ARCH SUPPORT DETAIL

STEEL STRIPS FOR TRAY AND GRILL

SEATING
SENSE

One of my prime rules of backyard design is that you should never be a slave to your valuable outside room. If you are a keen gardener, prepared to spend plenty of time on cultivation and maintenance, then that's fine. If you are not, a carefully designed composition will ensure you never have to spend more than a minimal amount of time looking after the space. But whether you are a keen gardener or a lazy one, sitting outside on a hot summer's day is one of life's great, simple pleasures. The choice of furniture is extensive, ranging from custom-made built-in designs to an almost unlimited variety of off-the-peg tables and chairs. The main consideration is that your choice reflects the underlying theme of the yard as a whole. While well-conceived moulded plastic chairs in primary colors can be great to sit in and look perfect in a modern design, they will appear quite awful in a period setting. In other words, think and look carefully before you buy or build, and if you are buying furniture always try it out. It's surprising how often a really elegant-looking chair can be appallingly uncomfortable.

Fine trees are often a focal point in a yard. A seat built around a tree will be visually attractive and will also benefit from the cool shade of a broad canopy of leaves.

While it is outside the abilities of the average home craftsman to build elaborate seating in metal or plastics, most projects that involve timber are well within reach, particularly if you take your time and carefully work out a sensible design beforehand.

Other objects and features in a garden often become occasional seats, and it may be worth taking this into account when choosing them. For example, the edge of a raised bed or pool approximately 18in. (45cm) off the ground is at a perfect height for perching, but if it's only one brick thick it won't be that comfortable. A double-brick wall, or one with a rounded brick coping or paving-slab top, will be altogether better. Such a feature will also be part of the overall composition and as such will fit comfortably within the design.

Built-in wooden seats can be both practical and attractive. They can be fitted into the angle formed by two house walls, built as an integral part of a barbecue area or form one or more sides of a wooden deck. The railroad ties that we looked at earlier for paving and raised beds (page 26) make ideal seats. Set them on sections of vertical railroad tie sunk into the ground, but make sure they are clean and not smothered with oil, which will make them totally unsuitable for use as seating in hot weather.

In a less formal situation large sections of fallen or felled tree trunks can be fashioned with a chainsaw to make a set of furniture. Chairs can be cut from single sections of wood and the table formed from a number of planks or, if the trunk is big enough, a large diameter slice.

One of the most attractive seating ideas I have seen, and something I am incorporating into my own yard, uses really large water-worn boulders. These must be substantial, so you will need mechanical means to shift them and partly bury them, but once in a carefully allocated position, close to or even surrounded by paving, they look quite superb. They also look good in an area of gravel and sculptural planting, but do need selecting personally from a stone merchant to get exactly the right shape and character.

As with the other elements of backyard design, avoid conflicting styles of furniture, and try to choose designs that are sympathetic to the overall look of your garden. Remember that painted finishes will require frequent retouching if they are not to become shabby.

Right: *A shady sitting area is often essential in a sunny garden, and this woodland retreat fits the bill perfectly. Both the seat and arbor are built from rustic wood, reflecting the backdrop and canopy of trees. The one element missing is the provision of a fragrant climber—honeysuckle, the traditional woodbine, would be the absolutely perfect choice.*

Right below: *Hammocks have a charm all their own, even if they are the very devil to get in and out of safely. Swinging gently beneath a shady branch is guaranteed to bring on a nap, but do make sure the limb of the tree is completely sound, otherwise you may fall to earth sooner than you had intended!*

Opposite: *This is definitely a set-piece sitting area. But for all that it is both practical and attractive: the brick steps and paving set it apart from the rest of the garden and the crisp outline of the seat stands out in sharp relief against the darker hedge. Planting is essential here to soften the architectural outline, the broad-leaved Plantain Lilys being a particularly effective touch.*

Just where you sit in the yard is another consideration and, while most patios are sited to catch the sun for much of the day, there is often a real need for a shady corner in which to relax. Such a sitting area can be an altogether smaller and quieter affair, probably positioned away from the house but linked back to it by a path. A backdrop of trees will often be enough to provide shade, but make sure you don't position a seat under a lime with its sticky drip.

Trees will also be the perfect hosts for a hammock, one of the most comfortable places for a quiet snooze. Do make sure the trunks are stout enough, though, and if you suspend the hammock from overhead branches, check them for any weakness or rot. Hammocks need to be of an ample size—the small ones are simply uncomfortable. They also take a deal of practice to get in and out of, often with a few tumbles in the process. Some hammocks come complete with stands, which is fine if you have no trees, but somehow that essential magic is lost.

While much furniture, including hammocks, is essentially static, it can be useful to have a number of light, folding chairs that can be moved around to chase sun or shade as the mood takes you, that can be tucked away in a minimal space for winter storage. Deck chairs were the traditional solution, and I think these still have a great deal of visual appeal. Equally comfortable and attractive are folding "director's" chairs. The fabric covers of such seats can pick up a color scheme used in the house if you will use them indoors as well as out, or provide the basis of a whole exterior color scheme, taking in awnings over windows, blinds, cushions, paint and even your planting arrangements.

Plastic furniture is reasonably priced and almost maintenance-free. While it can look a little stark, there has recently been a vast improvement in the quality and range of designs available. Again, the sympathetic use of fabrics will enable you to coordinate the furniture with your chosen planting scheme.

Exterior bean bags are one of the best new ideas I have seen. They consist of a water-repellent fabric filled with polystyrene granules. The size can be varied, but as a general rule the bigger the better. They are terrific for kids and adults alike and can be used just as well indoors.

TREE SEAT

A tree seat makes a charming focal point in a backyard. This octagonal seat sits comfortably around a tree trunk approximately 36in. (950mm) in diameter. But you should be able to adapt the measurements to fit the dimensions of your tree. If you build the seat to fit around a relatively young tree, remember to leave room to allow for growth and expansion of the tree trunk. Many nurseries now sell large tree specimens, and you might even consider buying and planting a suitable tree around which you could build this seat. The gently angled back follows the slope of the trunk, and the finished seat has been treated with a pale-colored, non-toxic wood preservative to extend its life. Depending on the layout of your yard and the location of the seat, you may want to treat it with a couple of coats of preservative and then paint it.

Finished lumber sizes vary considerably, so it is very important to measure as you work.

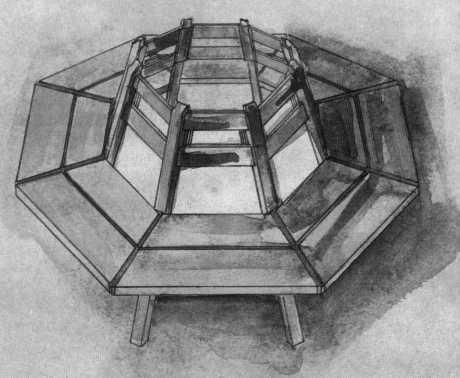

CONSTRUCTION

First, measure the circumference ("C") of the tree 18in. (450mm) above ground level. Now calculate the inner length of the inner seat board ("S") by multiplying "C" by 4 and dividing the total by 30; you can then calculate the total length of seat boards required by adding 6in. (150mm) to "S" and multiplying this new total by 24. The estimated total length of each row of backrest boards is simply "C" measured at its appropriate height (that is, at the height of the trunk where the bottom edge of the backrest boards will fall). However, this is only a guide to calculating the amount of lumber you will need to buy for the backrests; once the frames have been assembled and positioned around the tree, you will be able to measure the distance between the uprights to calculate the exact length.

Make a template, with angles as shown, cut from a 36 × 36in. (950 × 950mm) sheet of plywood to aid cutting major parts and to act as a pattern during assembly.

The first job is to cut the uprights to length using the template: cut the bottoms at an angle so the uprights will slope backward, notch out for the seat-support brace and rabbet the top for the backrest support. Mark the height of the spar (horizontal seat support) and shape the top of the upright. This detailing is just a nice finishing touch, and if you don't feel confident about shaping the top of the upright as shown, you could simply round off the front corner.

Place the spar on your template and mark and cut the angle necessary to fit the inside face of the spar flush against the upright.

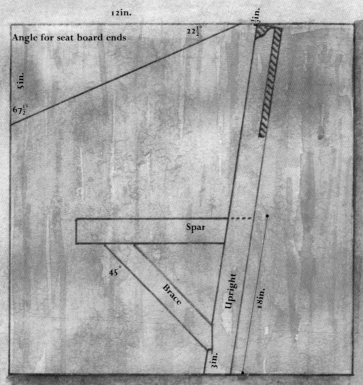

DRAWING UP A TEMPLATE

Use the template to mark a 22½-degree angle across the width of one of the seat board planks. Measure the hypotenuse, multiply by 3 (for three seat boards per section) and add 1in. (25mm), which will allow for the ½in. (12mm) spaces between each of the boards, to give the distance from the front to the back of the seat section.

Once you have calculated that measurement, position the upright and the spar on your template, then position the seat batten over the spar and mark a rabbet at one end of the seat batten to fit around the upright. Mark the front-to-back measurement of the seat section along from the bottom of the seat batten; cut the batten to length, angling the front end at 67½ degrees. Then cut a second seat batten that is the mirror image of the first.

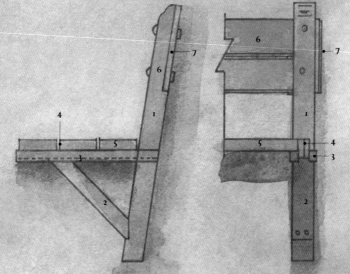

SIDE AND FRONT ELEVATIONS

KEY TO SIDE AND FRONT ELEVATIONS

1 Upright—3 × 3in. (75 × 75mm)
2 Brace—3 × 3in. (75 × 75mm)
3 Seat Batten—2 × 2in. (50 × 50mm)
4 Spar—3 × 2in. (75 × 50mm)
5 Seat Boards—$5\frac{1}{2} \times 1\frac{1}{4}$in. (138 × 32mm)
6 Backrest Boards—$5\frac{1}{2} \times 1\frac{1}{2}$in. (138 × 38mm)
7 Backrest Support—$5\frac{1}{2} \times 1\frac{1}{4}$in. (138 × 32mm)

CUTTING THE BRACE NOTCH
IN THE UPRIGHT

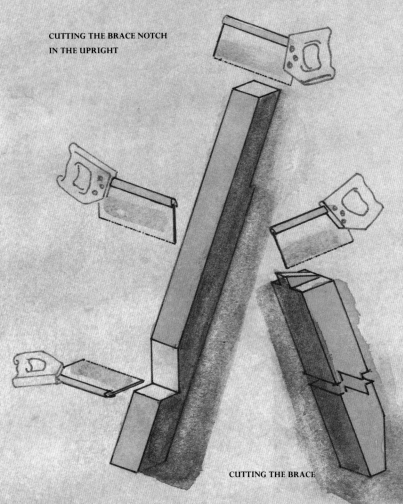

CUTTING THE BRACE

Place the spar between the two seat battens so that the back end of the spar is flush with the start of the rabbets and continue the angles from the front of the battens onto the front of the spar. Cut the front end of the spar so that it is V-shaped.

Next set the upright and the spar on the template to mark and cut the brace notches on each. The brace is notched into each by 1in. (25mm) at its deepest point. The brace can now be cut to fit in the notches. The top on both sides of the brace must then be rabbeted to hold the seat battens.

The backrest support can now be cut from $1\frac{1}{4} \times 5\frac{1}{2}$in. (32 × 138mm) softwood to the length of the two backrest boards plus the 1in. (25mm) gap between them; in this case, the backrest board is 12in. (300mm) long. Then chamfer the long edges of the support.

Cut all of the parts for the remaining seven frameworks. Carefully work around the pieces that you have already measured and cut for the first framework, and use them as templates for the corresponding parts. The project is now ready for assembly.

To assemble one of the seat sections, first attach backrest supports to two of the uprights using two carriage bolts and nuts per support. Glue and screw two of the seat battens to the spar, one on each side, so that the bottoms of the battens are flush with the bottom of the spar; use three brass countersunk screws for each batten. Stagger the screws and make sure they are positioned below the centers of the seat boards.

Glue and screw the brace into the notch you cut in the upright. Position the spar assembly on the

SHAPING THE ENDS OF
THE BACKREST BOARDS

brace and upright, and bolt the spar assembly to the upright with two heavy bolts. Screw through the brace and up into the spar.

Make five more frames in this way. The final two frames, for opposite sides, should be assembled without glue, but with heavy bolts securing the battens to the spar.

Although the front-to-back dimensions of the tree seat frames are pre-determined to take three seat boards per section, you will have to calculate the finished length of the slats yourself, since these depend on the size of the tree trunk around which you assemble the project. You have estimated this length already ("S"), but it is important that you check it accurately once the frames have been assembled and positioned.

Stand the eight frames around the tree, roughly in position and spaced apart at the required distance. Measure the length between two of the spars at the front of the uprights, and, back in your work space, mark this length (the revised, accurate "S") on one of the seat boards. Use the template to angle

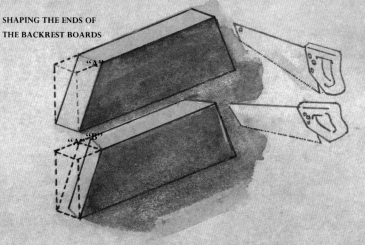

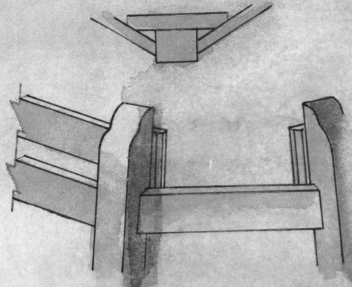

across the thickness of the board, mark point "B" $\frac{5}{8}$ in (16mm) in from "A" on the top back edge of the board. Join point "B" to point "A" on the top front edge and to the bottom back corner. Cut away the excess wood. Repeat with all the backrest boards. Cut them out and screw them to the backrest supports.

Sand off any sharp corners and make sure that the whole seat is well protected with nontoxic exterior-grade wood preservative.

the ends outward at $22\frac{1}{2}$ degrees and cut out the seat board. Position the seat board between the seat battens of two frames. Allowing for a $\frac{1}{2}$ in. (12mm) gap between the seat boards, measure the innermost lengths of the remaining two boards in this section, and angle the ends outward as before. Cut these two boards out and position them between the seat battens to check that all three boards fit accurately. If necessary, plane the edges of one or more of the boards so that they all fit snugly between the spars. You should then use these three boards as templates for all the others in the remaining sections (eight boards of each size).

Assemble the two sets of three seat sections, drilling, countersinking and screwing the seat boards down into the seat battens. It is important that you place the bolted spars and battens so that they will be on opposite sides when the seat is in position. If you wish to remove the seat, the battens can be unbolted from the spars. Mark on the ground the positions of the eight uprights.

It will be easier to level the seat if you dig holes—6in. (150mm) in diameter and 6in. (150mm) deep—at the upright positions, and fill them with gravel. This will also provide good drainage, reducing the risk of the uprights rotting. Take the two seat sections and place them in position around the tree; then screw the final two sections of seat boards down into the seat battens as for the other sections.

The backrest boards taper toward the top. The ends of all the boards also need to be angled across their width and their thickness. Measure the length of each board at its widest point between the uprights and cut it to this length. At both ends, measure 4in. (100mm) up from the bottom corner; at this point, measure $\frac{1}{4}$ in. (6mm) in from the edge. Join this point to the bottom corner, continuing the line up to the top edge ("A"). Mark point "A" on the opposite side of the top edge, draw a line down to the other bottom corner, and then cut out the triangle marked. To mark the angle

BASIC FRAME ASSEMBLY

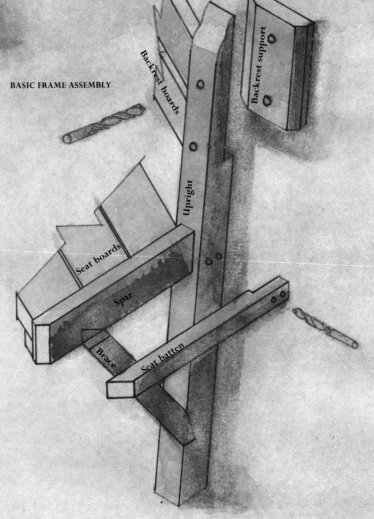

Backrest support

Backrest boards

Upright

Seat boards

Spar

Seat batten

Brace

Left: *Black iron hoops and the silver leaves of pyrus set up a fascinating dialogue that acts as a framework for the simple wooden seats below. Brick paving provides a mellow floor, while the shallow step sets the area apart from the rest of the yard.*

Opposite above: *Wicker is always a great favorite in a garden, the perfect color to tone with plants as well as being light enough to move around easily. Unfortunately the harsh creaking it sets up at the slightest movement is seldom conducive to a nap. That isn't a problem here as the seat is built from wood, the wicker acting as a shady bonnet.*

Opposite below: *In this unusual arbor, two mop-headed shrubs soften and front the vertical slats that form the main structure. Although the transition between light and shade is abrupt, there is enough dappled sun to prevent the composition from becoming somber in its effect.*

SUN AND SHADE

In tropical and subtropical countries the light is far brighter than in temperate zones. Designers in places such as the Mediterranean and the Middle East have understood and exploited the juxtaposition of light and shade for centuries, making full use of the high drama that is available in such situations. You have only to walk along a Spanish street or through an Italian garden to appreciate this, not only in tonal values but in terms of temperature, shade offering release from the sometimes overpowering heat. Even in more northern countries, where the sun is lower in the sky and the light is altogether softer, the juxtaposition of sun and shade can still be used in rather more subtle ways to contribute to the design and charisma of a yard. The placing of a tree part way down a lawn, so that a long shadow is cast across the area, tends to increase the feeling of space, the shadow acting as a threshold between two different areas. If those areas are handled in different ways or styles then the effect is reinforced. This is a visual division but with no physical barrier whatsoever.

In practical terms, you will almost certainly want some areas that are either in full sun or total shade, both for people and plants. While sunny areas simply require an open position, shady retreats will involve the creation of an area in shadow, by whatever means. An obvious choice is in the shade cast by a building or a group of trees, while a whole range of backyard constructions such as overhead beams, pergolas and arbors can produce rather more subtle effects as well as specific focal points within the garden framework.

In general terms the more open the framework the less dense the shade, and the dappled light cast in this way can often be the most attractive. The deeper the shade the greater the drama, a pool of darkness allowing an onlooker little idea of what is inside while for someone within quite the opposite applies.

These ideas show just how readily you can exploit the elements to provide another design tool at your disposal. Use the elements with sensitivity and you can add a new dimension to your palette, making sunshine and shadow work to your advantage in your garden planning.

ARBOR

This hexagonal arbor provides a delightfully shaded retreat in a corner of the backyard. The trellis at the back provides the perfect support for fragrant climbing roses, that have also scrambled over the roof. Such a building, of an open construction, offers little resistance to the wind, so it must be firmly secured to the ground. The hexagonal shape of the design calls for a lot of complicated angling of the component parts; the construction of this project is the most difficult in the book.

CONSTRUCTION

To set out a hexagon you will need to establish a center point of the building. Each corner will be 30in. (760mm) from the center; this will allow you to fit 24in. (605mm) wide panels of trellis to form the outside "walls." Each center angle of a hexagon is 60 degrees.

To plot the hexagon, mark a circle with a radius of 30in. (760mm) using a pencil or piece of dowel on a piece of string staked at the center of your plot. Choose any point on the circumference for the position of one of the posts, place the stake in the ground at this point, and draw another circle, again 30in. (760mm) in diameter, clearly marking the points at which it bisects the circumference of the original circle. Move the stake to one point and repeat the operation, until the six post positions have been marked.

The main upright posts are cut from 4 × 4in. (100 × 100mm) lumber and can be set into steel sockets bolted to a solid base or into spiked post-supports that are driven into the ground. Make sure the ready-made post-supports you buy have adjusting screws that allow the post to be checked vertically with a level and then clamped tightly in place. When driving spikes into the ground, always check first for any hidden services such as water pipes or electricity cables.

The uprights at the six corners of the arbor need to have slots in the top to accept the roof rafters. If you are unable to buy ready-made posts with slots in the top, mark out and cut a 2in. (50mm) wide slot, 4in. (100mm) deep, centered across one end of each of the six posts. Mark the width of the slot using a

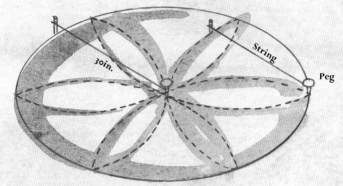

MARKING OUT THE SITE

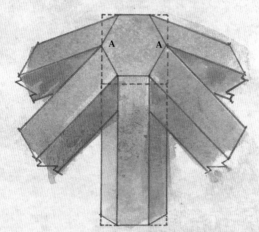

SHAPING THE CENTER POST

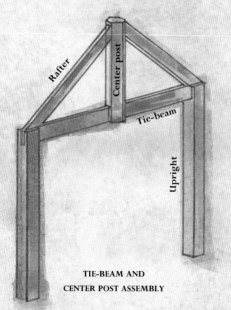

TIE-BEAM AND CENTER POST ASSEMBLY

marking gauge, saw down 4in. (100mm) using a tenon saw, and chisel out the waste. The upright posts should be approximately 7ft. (2.15m) high, but remember to allow for the depth of the fixing socket, if this is the method you are using. Nail 45-degree moldings along the lengths of the uprights to allow trellis panels to be attached. The moldings should run along the lengths of the posts, finishing just short of the bottoms to fit in the sockets or spiked supports. Glue and nail the moldings in place on both faces that have not had the slot cut down them, so that they finish about halfway across the width of the posts. Set the posts in the support sockets, with the moldings toward the "interior" of the arbor, and clamp together tight.

A tie-beam between two opposite uprights will give the building strength and stability. Cut the tie-beam to length from 2 × 4in. (50 × 100mm) with rabbets at each end to fit over the uprights. The tie-beam should span between two opposite uprights, finishing 1in. (25mm) short of the outside edges of the uprights. At each end of the tie-beam, cut a 1 × 3in. (25 × 75mm) rabbet and angle the ends above the uprights at 45 degrees to accept the rafters. Mark the center of the tie-beam on the bottom edge and secure with heavy bolts and nuts between the uprights.

Cut a notch in two of the rafters so that they will fit over the corner posts. Loosely bolt the rafters in position over the tie-beam, crossing at the apex. Support the pair of rafters with a C-clamp and set the angle of the rafters at 45 degrees to the tie-beam. Mark a line on both rafters where they cross over.

SHAPING THE RAFTERS

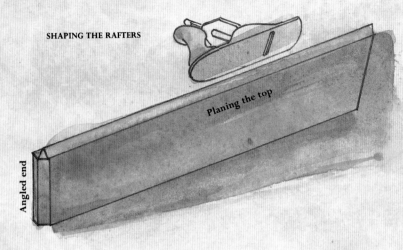

Planing the top

Angled end

Take the rafters down and mark vertical lines at the cross-over points; these will be at 45 degrees to the edges. Make sure that both rafters are marked to the same length and cut the vertical ends. Replace the rafters on the posts so that the vertical faces come together at the center. Measure from the bottom edge of the center of the tie-beam to the apex of the roof (where the rafters currently meet): cut the center post to this length.

Cut the center post to length from 4×4 in. (100×100mm). The center post needs to be shaped to a regular hexagon in cross section so that the rafters will neatly butt against it at the apex of the roof. Mark the position for a 2×2 in. (50×50mm) rafter centrally on one side of the center post. On the opposite side of the center post, mark a line $\frac{1}{2}$ in. (12mm) in from and parallel with the edge. Mark the position for a rafter centrally along this line. On the adjacent faces, mark a point $1\frac{3}{4}$ in. (43mm) along ("A" on Shaping the Center Post, page 49) and join this point first to the edges of where the first rafter will fall, and then to the point where the edges of the rafter will fall when you have sawn and planed away the waste $\frac{1}{2}$ in. (12mm). You should now have drawn the edges of a regular hexagon. Plane or saw the face angles so that the post is hexagonal in cross section. At the bottom of the center post, cut a slot to fit over the tie-beam, making sure that it runs between opposite flat faces.

Measure the distance between opposite faces of the center post and divide by two. Mark and cut this distance vertically, from the upper ends of the two rafters so that they butt onto the center post at the same angle.

Use these rafters to mark, cut and shape the remaining four rafters. Plane chamfers on the top edges and cut the bottom ends to a 120-degree V-shape so that the fascia boards (added later) will fit flush against the ends of the rafters.

Replace the rafters at each end of the tie-beam and position the center post on the center of the tie-beam, between the rafters. Nail through the rafters into the center post. Drill and bolt through the uprights into the rafters. Position a block on each side of the bottom of the center post and nail through the blocks into the

PLAN OF CORNER DETAIL

1 Trellis panel frame

2 Semicircular molding

3 45-degree molding

4 Slotted upright—
4×4 in. (100×100mm)

5 Tie-beam (angled at the end to accept the rafter)—
2×4 in. (50×100mm)

SECURING THE RAFTERS AND FASCIA BOARD

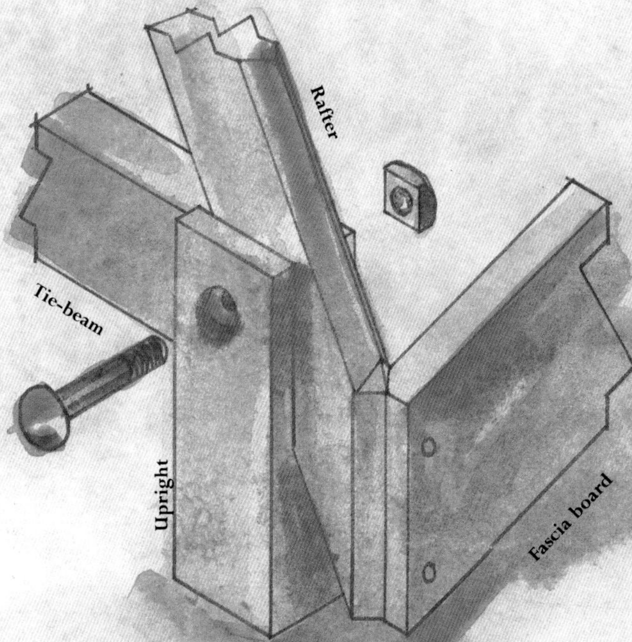

Rafter

Tie-beam

Upright

Fascia board

angles for the boards in situ, so that
they will fit from the center line of
one rafter to the next. Lay the
boards from the bottom upward,
pinning through the bottom of one
board into the top of the preceding
board it overlaps.

Such a pretty building as this
deserves a decorative top-knot: nail
a post cap and finial to the top of
the center post.

Chamfer the inside faces of the
trellis panel frames so that they fit
snugly between the 45-degree
moldings. Nail them in place and
cover the gaps at the outside corners
with semicircular moldings.

As an optional extra, you might
think of building a slatted seat
inside the arbor: screw 6in. (150mm)
angle brackets to the inner faces of
the uprights, and lay two 2 × 3in.
(50 × 75mm) boards between them.
Cut the ends of the boards to a 60-
degree angle so that they finish
square to the center line of the
corner posts, and screw them in
place. Treat all the surfaces with a
nontoxic, exterior-grade wood
preservative. Allow it to dry, then
paint or finish as desired.

ADDING THE ROOF BOARDS

Cut boards in situ

top of the tie-beam to keep the
center beam in place. Do not nail
the center post to the tie-beam.

The remaining rafters can now be
positioned, bolting them to the
uprights and nailing them to the
appropriate face of the center post.

Fascia boards surround the top of
the structure below the roof, and
these can now be cut to length.
Angle the ends at 60 degrees inwards
so that they butt neatly together.
Nail the fascia boards to the shaped
ends of the rafters.

The roof is clad in ½in. (12mm)
feather-edged boards pinned to the
rafters. You will need to chamfer the
undersides of the angled edges so
that each board abuts with those
on each side of it. Mark the cutting

PLAN VIEW OF ROOF

DECORATIVE DIVIDERS

*A yard, of whatever size, that can be seen at a glance is far
less interesting than one divided into separate areas.
As you move from space to space, the yard seems to unfold
with a satisfying element of mystery and surprise.
In all probability the area will also feel larger than it really is,
since you can spend time absorbing the character
of each component part before moving on to the next.
This technique has been used in the design of many great and
famous gardens and, although your backyard may be
considerably smaller, the principle remains much the same.*

*This simple, flower-laden trellis
sits on top of a low brick wall
that part-straddles the garden.
Such a divider is particularly
effective as it lets you catch
a tantalizing glimpse of the
"room" beyond, making it
all the more attractive.*

Right: *Gates may be enticing or welcoming; the character of the gate sets the theme. This strong wooden design, now beautifully mellowed with age, is distinctly rural and the old brick path and hedge reinforce the country garden feel. The positioning of a single white foxglove provides a point of emphasis, brightening the plain green foliage in the background.*

Far right: *Gardens don't have to be dull in winter. The tonal contrasts in this snow-covered yard are delicious and sharp. The gate invites you to explore beyond and creates a delicate filigree against the white lawn. The two yew buttresses capped with snow resemble Christmas puddings or ice-cream cones. Imagination is one of the great delights of gardening; make sure you use it.*

Space division within a yard is a vital tool in the creation of separate "rooms". Walls, screens and fences can be used in many ways to produce a variety of effects, so you should consider carefully what you want from your design. Two walls coming together to form a narrow opening will create a build-up of tension, or expectancy, as you approach the gap and a subsequent release, or feeling of surprise, as the next space is entered. A curving trellis, gently leading you through a garden but preventing you from seeing beyond the next corner, engenders mystery. A partly open gate is an invitation to find more.

Dividers can be constructed from various materials, and each has a character and suitability that makes it more or less appropriate for a given location. The choice is often confusing, given the vast range of options available, but certain guidelines, followed sensibly, will narrow down the options and ensure success.

One important rule is that the materials you use should reflect those used elsewhere in the composition. If your house is of brick or stone,

the natural choice, funds permitting, will be to use the same material in the yard. Although walls are expensive, if well built, on suitable foundations, and of adequate thickness, they will last for generations and be an ideal host for all kinds of climbing plants. Remember that, almost without exception, the real thing is better than an imitation. Reconstituted stone always looks just that, while the ubiquitous concrete "screen block" or pierced wall is appalling in most situations. The simplest things usually work best, particularly if the divider will not necessarily be seen as a feature in its own right but as part of a larger scheme.

Wood is a most versatile material and can be fashioned into the simplest fence or the most exotic trellis. Its lifespan is less than brick or stone, but if thoroughly coated with non-toxic preservative or bought already pressure-treated it will last for many years. Other advantages are its suitability for self-built projects and the relatively low purchase price. Weight, too, is a consideration: wood, being light, is an ideal

Far left: *A good feature in its own right can look quite out of place in the wrong setting. This sleek, modern trellis archway is, for my taste, at odds with the cottage feel of the herb and vegetable garden beyond. The chic formality of the trellis competes with the mellow, basketweave brick path—both beautiful features, but not complementary ones.*

Left: *Black, or dark colors, absorb light; white and other light colors actively reflect it, providing a much better screen. The shadow patterns set up by sunlight filtering through this trellis are delightful, while the hooped shape increases the apparent height of the feature. A hanging basket bursting with fuchsias draws attention to the curved ceiling and contrasts with the soft green of the ferns that are growing at ground level.*

choice for a roof garden, where it is a suitable material for screens that will filter rather than obstruct the wind, as well as for overhead beams and raised beds.

Hedges will be cheaper than both stone walls and wood but on the other hand, take longer to establish and need clipping to keep in shape. Having said that, once established, a well-tended hedge can provide a perfect "green wall'. Whether trimmed with a horizontal or curved top, or formed into balls or finials to emphasize a gateway, hedges act as one of the most attractive backdrops to planting, and their shape and height can be modified as you wish.

Of course, screens are not always simply decorative features. They can be used as practical devices to hide a utility area, store dustbins or form the boundary of the vegetable garden. Such screens should never be planned or positioned in isolation. It is better to extend them to link with the wider backyard pattern, so that problem areas are genuinely disguised without becoming eyecatchers in their own right.

Another way to make full use of dividers is to give them a dual or changing role. A stout wooden archway could start life as a child's swing, with access to the remainder of the yard temporarily re-routed. Later, when the swing is no longer needed, you could realign the path and let the feature take on a new character as a support for climbers. Such a scheme would be ideal in a small yard where play space might be limited. The requirements of a family yard change with the years and it is a good idea, therefore, to make versatility one of your prime considerations when you are planning a project.

Raised beds can also be used to create divisions and separate areas. They tend to act as lower-level barriers, although the contents of the bed will also affect the degree of screening. Raised beds can be used in many places, but are often most effective around the perimeter of a patio where they help to contain a space, or flanking steps that lead from one area to another. The hard edges of raised beds can be softened by growing plants that trail over the sides.

TRELLIS

Trellis, or treillage as it is sometimes pompously called, has a long pedigree as a garden feature. In its original form, it probably consisted of a woven screen of branches used for fencing or to support trained fruit trees against a wall. Today it is primarily used as a decorative element, but with careful planning you can combine this with the traditional approach to produce a very attractive screen, wind-break or base for climbing plants.

The most widely used type of trellis consists of thin strips of wood nailed together to form a diamond or squared pattern, but there are many other possibilities. Plastic is increasingly available and, if of good quality and simple design, can be quite acceptable. Wire, steel and wrought-iron have long been used in a variety of ways, ranging from strands of wire stretched between posts to delicate filigrees that reflect the architecture of an adjoining building. One of the great advantages of free-standing trellis is, of course, the ease with which it can be erected.

Pre-assembled trellis can be attached to posts that have been simply slotted into metal sleeves, or the posts can be spiked and driven into the ground or securely concreted into position. The initial cost may be high but, if regularly maintained, such a feature will last a life time.

A quick look at your local garden center will give you an idea of the enormous variety of trellis styles available. This is because trellis has become fashionable of late, so it is often used for that reason alone—an approach that seldom reflects good design sense. High fashion also comes with an expensive price tag, and many suppliers produce catalogs offering pseudo-bespoke designs that cost a small fortune. To justify the price, the patterns are often vastly complicated, and this makes them very difficult to fit into an overall backyard composition. There is, of course, a place for the complicated and intricate, but that place has to be reflected elsewhere in the design. Remember the prime rule that "simple things work best" and you will not go wrong.

One of the most common uses for trellis is as a support for climbers against a free-standing wall or against a house. In fact, wiring with horizontal strands is often more effective in this situation,

Simple white diamond trellis is the perfect foil to a fresh green climber, the underlying pattern providing background stability to the sun-speckled leaves.

Opposite above left: A white background to squared trellis appears to reduce the height of this wall, setting the upper limit of the "room". Such trellis is also an ideal support for potted plants, which can be hooked on to the horizontal slats.

Opposite above right: False-perspective trellis, or trompe-l'oeil as it is often called, seldom fools anyone—but it is fun. It is also the obvious focus for a well-chosen ornament such as this handsomely planted bowl.

Opposite below left: A simple free-standing device is an excellent host to any climber, either decorative or edible. The overall effect is charming and functional, the construction is minimal, and the fish above the apex of the triangular supports adds a restrained element of humor.

Opposite below right: When covered with planting, a divider like this one will prevent the eye from running the full length of a border, helping to create a feeling of suspense and drawing your view further down the yard. Instead of unwieldy fence posts, neat lengths of angle iron have been driven into the ground to support the panel ends.

costing less and involving little maintenance. Trellis may look better if it sets out to become a decorative element in its own right. Properly chosen and fitted, trellis will brighten and break the line of a dull wall. Make sure you align the tops of the panels with any obvious features such as windows or doors and remember that you will need to maintain it regularly, even when pre-treated timber is used. The plants which are growing against the trellis will have to be untied and any dead foliage cut away first. It can be difficult to remove climbers which have woven their way through the slats, and this may prove a maintenance problem.

Further down the yard, trellis can make an ideal screen, either in a decorative role, allowing you to catch a glimpse of what is beyond, or in a more practical way as a visual barrier to a utility or other area. The simplest pattern of trellis is often the best at hiding an unattractive view or feature. Climbers can be planted to complete the screen; if evergreens are chosen then the feature will remain effective and attractive even during the winter months.

Decorative screens can either be completely straightforward or rather more complicated. In an uncluttered, domestic yard a basic squared pattern of strong trellis will be ideal. This style is excellent for climbers and will easily withstand the wear and tear caused by children and teenagers playing ball in the garden. It could extend part way across the space or include an archway to the area beyond. In the context of a more stylized and formal yard, there is justification for a more complex pattern. Here, a trellis could follow shapes used elsewhere, with curved tops, hooped arches or close-set slats combined in any number of ways. Remember, too, that trellis is internationally used. Superb styles have been developed in Japan, the Far East and other parts of the world, extending the vast catalog of design possibilities.

Another practical approach to screens and dividers is to use them as wind-breaks. Very often a solid fence or wall will create wind turbulence on the lee side. In contrast, slats or trellis tend to filter the wind effectively with no such disadvantages. This facility can be exploited both at ground level and in a roof garden, which is where trellis will really come into its own.

Far left: *Trellis need not simply be used for dividers and screens in the further reaches of the yard. Here it makes a simple but effective support for climbers around a porch. A design like this one casts little shadow and provides an attractive and simple welcome to the house.*

Top left: *Close-mesh diamond trellis is the ideal boundary for a rooftop garden. It is lightweight and will filter the wind far more effectively than a solid structure. In this design the pattern has been continued in the raised bed, with planting chosen to soften the outline.*

Bottom left: *This custom-built design in well-made, solid wood is the perfect divider between two outdoor "rooms". The squares are slightly larger than usual and combine well with the hooped pattern that gives the feature a real feeling of movement. Climbers and planting at a lower level have been well chosen, tempering the architectural line of the screen.*

BACKYARD SCREEN

This divider is cheap and easy to build, provides an increasingly effective screen for the building opposite as the climbers develop, accentuates the slight change of level and finally separates the more formal part of the yard from the lawn.

Attached to the exterior wall of a house, the divider works as an architectural link between inside and outside, but it could be modified so that it is a freestanding unit in a more informal part of the yard. The rabbet in the top rail above the left-hand intermediate post is not essential because the wall bracket provides rigidity, but if the feature is freestanding, then all the posts must be rabbeted into the top rail.

The size of this divider could be varied to suit individual situations; in this backyard it is approximately 6ft. 6in. (2m) high.

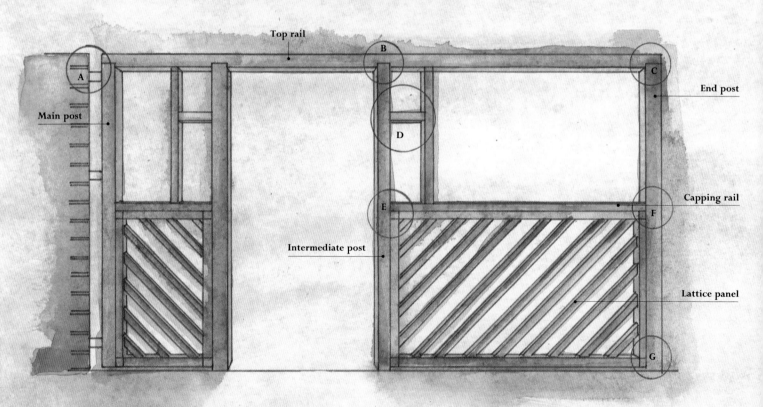

Top rail

A

B

C

End post

Main post

D

Capping rail

E

F

Intermediate post

Lattice panel

G

CORNER OF
LATTICE PANEL (F)

END POST AND
TOP RAIL (C)

CONSTRUCTION

First construct the frame for the diagonal lattice from 2 × 2in. (50 × 50mm) softwood with halving joints at the corners. Check that the frames are square, and glue and nail them together.

Mark out the position of the slats on the framework with about a 3in. (75mm) spacing between each. Cut the slats to length with a 45-degree angle at each end (mark the angle

INTERMEDIATE POST AND TOP RAIL (B)

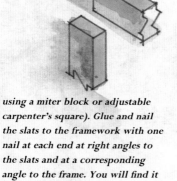

using a miter block or adjustable carpenter's square). Glue and nail the slats to the framework with one nail at each end at right angles to the slats and at a corresponding angle to the frame. You will find it easiest to work from opposite corners toward the center.

Offer up the main post to the wall of the house, check the vertical and mark the position for three expanding masonry bolts. Remove the post and bore the holes in it. Offer up the post again and mark the position of the holes on the masonry. Drill these using a masonry bit to a depth slightly greater than the distance the bolt will penetrate the wall. Bolt the post to the house,

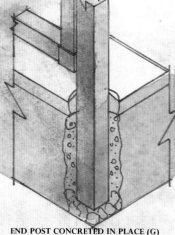

END POST CONCRETED IN PLACE (G)

fitting spacers to keep the upright slightly away from the building.

Cut the top rail to the right length: that is, so that it will span the length of both lattice panels, the archway and the four posts. Cut rabbets to fit the posts into the rail.

Position the top rail at the base of the fixed post to mark the position of the other end post on the ground. Cut a gauge batten the same length as the top rail, minus the width of two posts and mark on it the intermediate post positions.

Use a post-hole borer or posting spade to excavate for the

intermediate posts and the end post. Cut the end post so that 18in. (450mm) will be set in the ground and set the post on a 4in. (100mm) layer of well-compacted gravel. Prop the post upright with long battens set on two adjacent sides. Set the top rail in position to check that the spacing is correct at the top; check the spacing at the bottom using the gauge batten.

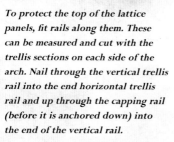

VERTICAL AND HORIZONTAL
TRELLIS RAILS (D)

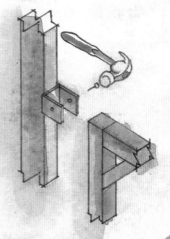

NAILING LATTICE PANEL TO
FENCE BRACKET (E)

Cut intermediate posts to length, fill the holes with 4in. (100mm) of gravel, check the post heights and prop upright. Concrete the posts in position, bringing the surface slightly above ground. Allow two or three days for it to dry and remove the supporting props.

Nail or screw fence-post brackets to the inside faces of the pairs of posts, even with the top and bottom of the diagonal lattice panels. The bottoms of the panels should be just clear of the ground. It is then a simple matter to slide the panels up into the brackets at the top and then ease them down into the bottom ones. Nail the panels in place.

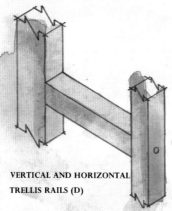

To protect the top of the lattice panels, fit rails along them. These can be measured and cut with the trellis sections on each side of the arch. Nail through the vertical trellis rail into the end horizontal trellis rail and up through the capping rail (before it is anchored down) into the end of the vertical rail.

Nail through the top rail and intermediate posts into the ends of the trellis rails and through the capping rail into the lattice panel top frame.

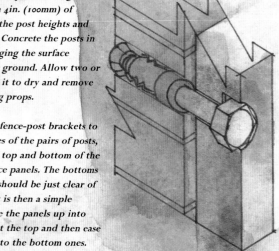

BOLTING MAIN POST TO WALL (A)

Left: *An arch or pergola should always be integrated with the design of the yard. This simple arrangement frames a grass path that in turn has a statue as a focal point at the end. The arch is all the more telling as it sets up a visual dialogue with the rose-garlanded rope swags.*

Opposite: *This gloriously unkempt combination of path and pergola has in fact been very carefully designed to lead both foot and eye through a cool tunnel towards the informal steps and sunlit turf beyond. The square wooden supports are topped by simple poles that span the walkway and provide support for fragrant roses climbing up and overhead. The apparently haphazard planting simply heightens the intended effect of a delightful rural idyll.*

PERGOLAS

Pergolas are one of the oldest landscaping elements. Their history can be traced back to the very earliest representations of cultivation in Egyptian courtyards. Their role was a dual one: to support the twining stems of vines and to provide a degree of shelter from the all-pervading sun. Since then, pergolas, tunnels, and arches have been incorporated into many different types of yards, but it is worth remembering that a pergola is primarily a vehicle for plants. Climbers in particular often thrive on a pergola, growing far better than they do when planted close to the house, where their growth is hindered by foundations, poor soil or the lack of moisture caused by an adjoining wall's "rain shadow".

In contemporary design terms, a pergola will tend to be a dominant element, particularly in a relatively small space, and its positioning and method of construction will play an important part in the overall design pattern. The height and shape of a pergola make it naturally attractive, so it should be sited to draw both foot and eye in a particular direction. If it is built to follow the curve of a path, the far end will disappear with an air of mystery. If it is straight, the focal point might be a well-chosen statue, an urn, or a seat. Whatever the focus and wherever the destination, it should be positive—a pergola placed at random is simply wasted space.

Styles and methods of construction vary enormously, from simple wooden affairs, through complicated brick, stone, or tile piers to metal arches that are virtually hidden when garlanded with climbers. As with paving and walling, the theme should be taken from the surrounding environment. A brick-built pergola adjacent to a stone cottage would look incongruous. In a contemporary setting, a modern pergola will be appropriate. I recently designed a superb pergola from a series of hoops of large-diameter tubular stainless steel. The final effect of the metal glittering through a tracery of foliage was incredibly dramatic, confirming my belief that, ancient or modern, a properly used and sensitively sited pergola will always be an indispensable element in a good design.

VINE SUPPORT

This feature is genuinely versatile and could act as a screen at the corner of a patio, a container on a terrace or set as a pair to flank the entrance to a vegetable patch. Even a moderate wind could easily topple a structure this tall, so stability is extremely important, and the main posts must be driven firmly into the ground.

CONSTRUCTION

Level the site and mark out the position of the trough, using pegs driven into the ground at the corners and at the positions of the intermediate posts. Join together with twine, making sure corners are at right angles. Bore holes for the two main upright posts 18in. (450mm) deep, or drive in 24in. (600mm) long steel post sockets. Always check for the position of any underground services such as water pipes or electricity cables.

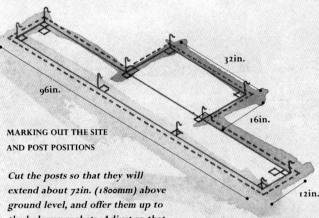

MARKING OUT THE SITE AND POST POSITIONS

Cut the posts so that they will extend about 72in. (1800mm) above ground level, and offer them up to the holes or sockets. Adjust so that the tops of the post are level.

Remove the posts from the holes and lay them down flat, spaced at the distance they will be when erected. Lay the bottom support batten at the bottom of the posts with an equal overlap at each end and mark the position of the inside faces of posts on the batten. These marks can then be transferred centrally to the cross beams for the top of the posts. Drill countersunk clearance holes for No. 12 screws in the cross beams staggered on the posts and $1\frac{1}{2}$in. (38mm) from the top and bottom edges of where the cross beams will be positioned.

Angle the post top at 45 degrees so water will easily run clear.

Line up the post marks on one cross beam against the two posts, and clamp the cross beam to the posts using C-clamps so the top is flush with the post top. Drill pilot holes and screw the cross beam to the posts using two $2\frac{1}{2}$in. (62mm) No. 12 brass countersunk screws at each end. Repeat for the other beam.

Drill countersunk clearance holes at 24in. (600mm) centers in the top string support batten. Make a template from a scrap of $\frac{1}{4}$in. (6mm) plywood to mark the nail positions.

Use slightly blunted $1\frac{1}{2}$in. (38mm) galvanized nails, and drive these in a staggered pattern so the batten is not split. Screw the batten centrally to the front cross beam, $\frac{1}{2}$in. (12mm) up from the bottom edge using $2\frac{1}{2}$in. (60mm) No. 8 brass countersunk woodscrews.

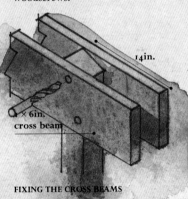

FIXING THE CROSS BEAMS

Stagger nails or screws into the bottom string support as above. Mark the ground level on the posts. Screw the batten centrally to the front of the posts, 10in. (250mm) above ground level. Use $2\frac{1}{2}$in. (60mm) No. 8 brass countersunk screws to do this.

Knot garden twine or plastic wire between the top and bottom nails.

Lift the frame into the holes or sockets and set in concrete or tap home as appropriate.

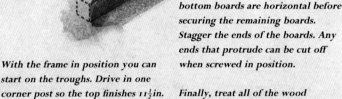

3 × 3in. post   FIXING THE STRING SUPPORT BATTENS

With the frame in position you can start on the troughs. Drive in one corner post so the top finishes $11\frac{1}{2}$in. (285mm) above ground level. Check the vertical and drive in the remaining corner and intermediate posts to follow the lines marked out with pegs. Level the tops from the first post using a straightedge and level. Check that the lower string support batten does not protrude beyond the end corner posts.

Screw the boards for the troughs to the corner posts and intermediate posts with $2\frac{1}{2}$in. (60mm) No. 8 brass screws, two per post. Check that the

bottom boards are horizontal before securing the remaining boards. Stagger the ends of the boards. Any ends that protrude can be cut off when screwed in position.

Finally, treat all of the wood thoroughly with two coats of a nontoxic wood preservative.

SCREWING TROUGH BOARDS TO THE CORNER POSTS

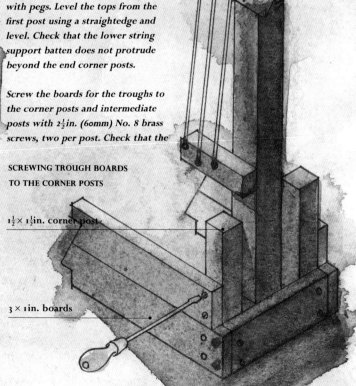

$1\frac{1}{2}$ × $1\frac{1}{2}$in. corner post

3 × 1in. boards

RAISED BEDS

I'm essentially a lazy gardener and if there is a way to tend plants at a comfortable height, rather than at ground level, then I'm all for it. But this is just one of the advantages of raised-bed gardening. Raised beds give young plants a much-needed boost, soften the hard line of an adjoining wall, double as occasional seats, become an integral part of steps or ramps, or temporarily provide a children's sandpit. You can use them to contain a given area such as a patio or vegetable garden. Remember that the soil in a raised bed can be quite different from that in another part of the garden. This will allow you to grow plants that would not normally thrive in the immediate vicinity—for example ericaceous plants could be grown in an acidic bed in an otherwise chalky garden.

Opposite above left: This stone raised bed forms part of a rockery and fulfils its function perfectly, elevating the delicate alpine planting to a handy working height and also bringing it closer to eye-level.

Opposite above right: Railroad ties are ideal for backyard construction. They're easy to lay and almost indestructable—but don't try to move them alone as they're very heavy and need a person at either end for easy lifting. Here, the contrast in color between the dark wood and the lighter gravel path is particularly effective.

Opposite below: Railroad ties have been cut into short sections and set vertically to form an attractive bed. Burying approximately 50 percent of the length below ground level makes the feature immensely strong. Varying the height of the tops sets up an interesting rhythm, with plants arranged to blur the outline.

To exploit their full potential, you should consider the option of raised beds during the initial stages of creating your design. Where you decide to put them will of course have a bearing on the materials you use for their construction. A brick raised bed could echo brick paving, which in turn takes its cue from the house. Stone will combine well with stone, wood with wood and so on. But this is only a guide and these rules can be broken. Neatly laid railroad ties look superb in a contemporary setting adjoining a house built from brick. Similarly, rendered concrete blocks with a neat precast slab coping would offer an immediate visual affinity with a stuccoed building.

If beds are built with solid brick or stone walls then drainage will be necessary to prevent the soil from becoming waterlogged. You can leave a number of open vertical joints close to the ground to allow excess water to seep away. Alternatively, drainage pipes can be neatly incorporated at a similar level, but make sure that they finish flush with the face of the wall. As with any wall, suitable concrete foundations are essential. Most importantly, a raised bed should never be built directly on top of existing paving. Remember, too, that raised beds may cause damp problems if built against a house wall. Always leave a gap between a bed and an adjoining wall.

Wood is an excellent choice of material and very versatile. Beds can utilize logs set vertically into the ground or laid horizontally, nailed into supporting battens or posts set into the ground on the inside of the bed. Large wooden plant boxes, constructed from boards and filled with lightweight compost, will be ideal for roof gardens, where weight considerations mean that heavier materials are not suitable.

Left: This curved brick wall with a neat stone coping echoes the brick paving used in the patio. The smothering flowers and foliage soften the effect and inject an element of contrast. Such a raised bed could exist alone or make up part of an altogether larger scheme of retaining walls and different levels.

Right: *In this classic combination, hedge and gate sit comfortably together, the sharp pickets seeming to push the green arch up and away from the entrance. A hedge like this takes a while to establish and needs careful clipping and training during its development, but the end result is worth it and would provide a real welcome to any yard.*

Opposite above: *Fence, screen, or both—the definition hardly matters as this is a delightful way to divide the space. White roses provide a perfect contrast, sparkling against the soft green background. It is worth remembering that, while rustic timbers look fine in the more distant parts of a garden, they may appear uncomfortable if situated close to the house, particularly as they have a limited life-span and tend to rot.*

Opposite below: *Ivy covers this brick wall, growing tightly against the surface and needing minimal maintenance to keep it neat. Holes clipped in the foliage introduce a textured effect with a contrast between light and shadow. The ivy-clad birdbath is also very effective: you need to look twice to see how it works.*

FENCES, GATES, AND HEDGES

Fences and hedges can form either internal divisions or the external boundaries of your plot. Gates will always be the ins and outs of a yard. As with many of the other elements of the design, the range of options is enormous, but here again your choice should reflect the general style of the surrounding composition so that the development of your yard has continuity.

In many cases the choice between a fence and a hedge can be an entirely subjective one. A fence is quickly erected, offers immediate screening and has an average life of between 10 and 15 years. Options can range from the soft texture of woven stems of hazel or willow to the austerity of a purpose-designed pattern of carefully shaped and spaced slats. There will certainly be a requirement for maintenance, either by regular painting or treatment with a non-toxic preservative. Cost will vary, but any fence, even if home-built will involve a considerable outlay both in materials and in labor. This being the case, it is important to consider all the possibilities when planning the fencing most suitable for your yard.

Hedges are initially far cheaper to buy and plant, but will take several, or in some cases many, years to reach maturity and provide an adequate screen. In visual terms they offer a far softer appearance than a fence or wall and often provide the perfect backdrop to planting, seating or statuary. Because you are dealing with a living material, the appearance of a hedge will change with time, while, of course, it can be trained or clipped into a variety of patterns and shapes. Topiary is a fascinating art, and the element of humour it adds to a garden design is invaluable. Remember, though, that a lot of maintenance is required to keep a clipped shape, with its crisp edges, looking trim, but that this is essential if the impact of your topiary is not to be lost.

Gates provide a natural focal point at the end of paths and paving. The choice is legion, ranging from a low, open structure of woven iron to a full-height wooden door that will exclude the view completely. Choose carefully, remembering that gates are often the first thing that visitors see – and first impressions count.

WATER FEATURES

*Water has a magic all its own—from the strict formality
of a rectangular pool set within paving and sculptural planting,
to the sweep of an irregularly shaped pond that sets up
reflections of everything around it.
Imagine the crash of a waterfall onto rocks below
or the gentle murmur of a fountain in a raised bed. The mood of
water changes too: steel gray, sharp and rimed with frost
in the depths of winter; deliciously cool and
framed with aquatic planting in the warmth of summer.
Of course, water features are not just appreciated by us: a pool
is one of the richest habitats you can create in your yard.
Birds and insects will come to drink, the frogs and
toads that are great predators of unruly bugs will thrive,
marginals and deep water plants will bring their own exotic
charm, while fish complete the picture.
More than any other feature, water will echo your personality.
Just how you handle it will be a subtle challenge –
success brings enormous pleasure.*

*This circular pool is a natural
focus in a courtyard setting. It is
raised, bringing it closer to
eye-level and making it a good
deal safer for young children.
It's also at a perfect height for
sitting on, while the blue brick
coping matches that used in
the surrounding raised beds.*

Since a water feature can be the making or breaking of a yard, you should plan it carefully. As with other areas of design, the simple things invariably work the best. I so often visit gardens where a "Geneva" fountain gushes high into the air from a quite minuscule pond. Apart from being completely out of scale, the combination is totally impractical, as spray drift results in an alarming rate of water loss in even the lightest of winds.

The style of a pool should reflect the character of the area around it. A pond set within a patio can be built from the same material as the paving, interlocking, perhaps, with a raised bed or set within the angle of a wall. The further away from the house you get, the softer and looser the composition can become, and this change can be reflected in the shape of the pool.

The situation with regard to sun and shade will also be important. Try to find a position well out in the open, away from the shadow and leaf fall of overhanging trees. If leaves are a problem—and neighbors' trees are often to blame as much as yours—then spread a light net over the pool at the onset of autumn. You can then remove the whole lot once they have all fallen.

In the ideal pool there is such a balance of aquatic plants, fish, water snails, and a host of other insect life that the fish hardly ever need feeding. There are now specialist water garden centers where you can buy all that is necessary to bring your pool alive. If you let them know the size and depth of your pool they will work out the correct permutations, down to the last water snail that will help to keep the water clear. The smaller the area the more difficult it is to create a balanced habitat. The minimum size for a pool is 6 × 6ft. (1.8 × 1.8m), while 18in. (450mm) is an adequate depth. You will also need a shelf or ledge, approximately 9in. (220mm) below the surface and about 12in. (300mm) wide, on which to stand marginal plants.

In the past all garden pools were made from concrete. This made them time-consuming to create and fraught with the problems of hair-line cracks. Tough plastic and butyl liners have provided the solution and are now available in virtually any size and in many different grades. An alternative option is to choose a rigid or semi-rigid pool. But, although these can be quickly and easily installed, they are often rather too small to be really effective.

FORMAL PONDS

A formal pattern suggests symmetry in which one side or part of a yard or design is identical to the other. While this is not always strictly true, we tend to think of a formal design as one that is built up from geometric elements rather than free-form shapes, displaying a strong degree of visual control and stability.

As far as pools are concerned, the geometry can be square, rectangular, circular, triangular, or even a combination of these elements. Formal ponds are usually surrounded by a coping of some kind, even if they are set within an area of soft landscaping in the form of lawn or planting. They may form a set-piece within the larger setting of a courtyard, sunken garden, or parterre, and will associate particularly well with decorative features such as statuary, topiary, or regularly-placed urns and ornaments.

You may want to use an ornament as the centerpiece of the pool itself. Figures engaged in some sort of watery activity are very popular, as are bowls from which water overflows back into the pool below. Where a pool is backed by a wall there is the opportunity to fit a mask that also spouts water. Lions' heads are the most common, but are rarely modeled well and tend to become a design cliché. Instead try and seek out something different: a gargoyle or a face of some other kind could be a better choice and could inject a humorous touch into the formality of the composition. As well as being visually pleasing, a fountain or cascade adds a further dimension to the attractions of a formal pool, with the sound of falling water providing a soothing background to backyard activities. A variety of effects can be produced, depending on the type of fountain jet or head fitted.

Any pond including a fountain or cascade will require a pump. Today there is a wide range of submersible types available that are easily fitted within the pool itself. Many work from a 12 volt supply that is connected back to a transformer inside the house or garage. When using electricity in the yard, and particularly near water, make absolutely sure that all connections are of the correct weatherproof type, and employ a qualified electrician to install the pump so that you can be absolutely sure that it is safe.

Opposite above: *In design terms a square is completely static and as such makes an ideal centerpiece in a formal situation. The effect of this pool is heightened by the stepped brickwork that leads the eye down to the water. The hummocks of box, the carefully positioned pots, seat and trained ivy all add to the overall geometric arrangement of this well-planned area.*

Opposite below: *A water-filled bowl and fountain draw the eye to the center of this composition. Crisp brick paving surrounds the pool which is in turn softened by the formally placed beds and the dense evergreen background. If you are planning to use a bowl in this way you should first make sure that it is completely frost-proof and able to withstand the ravages of winter.*

Left above: *A tiny circular pool introduces a note of formality in an otherwise rural yard. Well-laid coping acts as a mowing edge to the surrounding lawn, but the lily plants will need thinning regularly if they are not to overrun the pool area completely.*

Left below: *Fountains and bubble jets are fine, but you will never enjoy the beauty of reflections from such a disturbed surface. A large formal pool like this is all the more effective for being perfectly still. The surrounding path here is wide enough for a wealth of low-growing and alpine plants, some in pots and some planted in cracks within the paving. The whole feature is part of a larger design forming the focal point of a sunken area of grass and planting.*

INFORMAL PONDS

Natural ponds are invariably informal. If you want to create something similar in your own yard you should first study how water looks without the interference of man. For a start, it will almost certainly be situated in a fold or dip in the land and, although we don't always have that much space at home, we can at least use the shapes and contours of the land to ensure that the feature sits comfortably in its surroundings. You can use the dirt from the excavation for this contouring. Remember to keep the topsoil separate from the subsoil, replacing it last as a medium for planting or lawn.

Since natural ponds do not have any kind of artificial lining, one of the worst blunders in building an informal pool is to leave the edge of a butyl sheet or concrete rim projecting above the water. The secret is, of course, to lay the liner beneath the bank, bringing it up above the water level a short way from the edge of the pool. The sides of the pool should, if possible, dip gently towards the water with marginal planting linking the two elements together. Alternatively, a beach of cobbles or small stones can be a most effective edge and will allow animals to approach and drink more easily.

Planting is vitally important both in and around a natural pond. On a very grand scale, trees, particularly weeping trees, will provide a strong vertical line against the horizontal plane of water. Willows are quite magnificent if you have a garden and lake of many acres, but are a disaster in a small plot. Far better is weeping birch or one of the larger shrubs such as dogwood or bamboo.

I'm very much against the use of brash fountains in informal ponds. Reflections are far more telling: if a pool can be sited so that it mirrors a wide open sky or a particularly fine area of planting, then your design is almost guaranteed to be a success. In a rural situation, you might even occasionally have the opportunity of using water as a boundary, drawing the more distant landscape into the yard. In this instance, a fence becomes superfluous and you can enjoy that rare and precious element—an uninterrupted view of the open countryside beyond.

Opposite above: *One of the great joys of having a pool is being able to walk across it. Some bridges are pretentious and ghastly, an unfavorable reflection of the character of the owner. Far better, as here, to have a simple wooden structure that is softened by the generous planting.*

Opposite below: *I suspect this pond started life as a formal composition, but somebody who loves plants got hold of it and obliterated the geometric lines. To my mind this is the right approach: formality is there to be tempered—and what a haven this must be for wildlife.*

Right: *This stunning combination of irises and primulas provides a splash of vibrant color against the darker background of shrubs. The banks of the pool disappear into the shadows while the lily pads provide shade and shelter for the fish and other pond life.*

RAISED POND

A raised pond is both an attractive and a practical feature in a backyard, and this one is the perfect height to double as a seat. However, as with all water features, safety must be paramount, and if you choose to build a pond, then do make sure it is child-safe.

The pond shown here is 72in. (1800mm) long, 54in. (1350mm) wide and approximately 12in. (300mm) high. The exterior surfaces are clad in slate, although you could use paving or natural stone materials; the important consideration is to match the cladding to the paving.

CONSTRUCTION
Prepare a sound base. On a solid concrete surface this will involve very little work, but in a yard make sure that the surface is level and excavate suitable foundations or footings. These must be twice as wide as the walls and approximately 12in. (300mm) deep. Check the depth of the footings all around and drive stakes into the bottom of the trench so that they are just below ground level, making sure they are level. Fill the trench with concrete up to the height of the stakes.

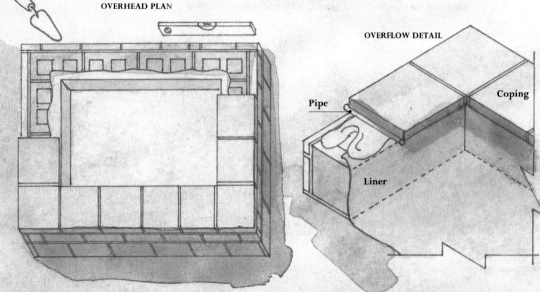

SETTING OUT THE BASE

9 × 9 × 18in. block

Leave the concrete to set for two days; then skim off any soil that has settled on the foundations. Remove any sharp stones that could damage the pool liner.

Build the walls from a single course of hollow concrete blocks. Mark out lines using chalk, checking the corners are at right angles using a 3:4:5 triangle. You should build the pool to a size that avoids having to cut the blocks.

Lay a $\frac{3}{8}$in. (10mm) bed of mortar along one long side between chalk lines, and lay a single course of blocks with mortar between each. Check that the course is level and true. Remove any surplus mortar and make sure the joints are flush on the inside faces.

Repeat the process to lay the first course for both of the short sides and then the second long length.

Set out the cladding dry for each side, allowing sufficient overlap at one end to butt the next side up to it. Work your way along the face of one side; then carry out any necessary cutting when you get to the corner. Set the cladding on the face of the concrete blocks with mortar so that it finishes flush with the top. A crisp rectangular material, such as slate, can be closely butt-jointed, but any joints that show should be neatly rubbed back.

OVERHEAD PLAN

Clean up the inside faces of the concrete blocks and remove any sharp protrusions or edges that could damage the pond liner. Lay a sheet of liner underlay and anchor it with builders' tape.

Lay a $\frac{3}{8}$in. (15mm) layer of soft sand over the base of the pool to cushion the pond liner. The size of liner should be twice the depth of the pool plus the overall length, and twice the depth of the pool plus the overall width. Lay the liner over the pool walls, ease it into place and loosely anchor it with half a dozen slabs around the edges.

Fill the pool with water to within 1in. (25mm) of the top. The liner will stretch and mold to the exact profile of the walls. Trim the excess liner, leaving a $1\frac{1}{2}$in. (40mm) fringe that can be secured under the coping. Any wrinkles should be folded so they lie flat.

The coping should be the same material as the cladding. Lay it out around the pool prior to bedding in the mortar so the coping can be cut

to fit. The coping should overhang the inside of the pond by 2in. (50mm) to help hide the liner.

Lay the coping on a $\frac{3}{8}$in. (10mm) bed of mortar. A useful precaution against the pond's overflowing is to bed a section of $\frac{5}{8}$in. (15mm) diameter plastic pipe across the mortar, so that it runs between the inside and outside faces of one wall. Lay the coping above the pipe, checking that is level.

OVERFLOW DETAIL

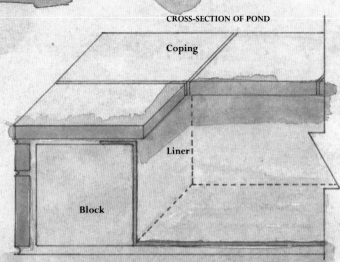

Pipe

Coping

Liner

CROSS-SECTION OF POND

Coping

Liner

Block

ELEMENTS OF DESIGN

As in other parts of the yard, the overall concept and make-up of a pond can be split into the elements of hard and soft landscape. The method of construction and certain features will fall under the former while the planting, fish, insect, and other life will follow on as a natural second stage to complement the size, position, materials, and style chosen for the pool.

I have already mentioned the differences between concrete and liner construction, emphasizing the advantages of the latter being made from material that is better suited to prolonged contact with water.

In most instances, and certainly in formal pools, the liner will need anchoring in some way. This is usually done with a coping that surrounds the pool. The range of copings is wide but your choice should, if possible, take its cue from materials used elsewhere in the garden. If you have a terrace or patio constructed from stone slabs then your pool could use a similar coping. The same would apply to brick, slate, or concrete paving. Preformed fiberglass pools should also be fitted with a coping to disguise the edge—brick often conforms best to the convoluted shapes of many of the free-form types. For durability and safety the coping should be securely bedded on mortar. If a pool is situated within a lawn area then the coping should be set slightly below the level of the turf so that a mower can run smoothly over the top.

Lighting can add an altogether new dimension to a pool at night. There are a number of easy-to-install kits available. Safety is of paramount importance, so if in doubt, employ the services of a qualified electrician. Some pool lighting is appalling, particularly the floating, rotating, multicolored displays that seem designed to induce a headache in double-quick time. Stick to white and blue bulbs, which are both the most natural and the most effective. Bulbs in these colors will enhance the appearance of the foliage growing in and around the water rather than detract from it, and can be used in conjunction with other areas of lighting around the yard. Simplicity and subtlety are the keys to success, otherwise the resulting illuminated scene will merely look contrived.

Lily pads are one of the most satisfying elements of a pond, but need water that is about 24in. (600mm) deep. The more rampant varieties of lily will also require regular thinning.

Opposite above left: A well-balanced pool will always have frog potential and they should be encouraged. It's fascinating, particularly for children, to watch tadpoles develop, while adult frogs are an enormous help with pest control in the garden.

Opposite above right: Rock often associates well with water, but only if it is used in as natural a way as possible. Each piece should be set at the same angle, along a "bedding plane." Marginal planting, set in baskets on a shelf below the water, brings the composition to life and softens the somewhat austere rock backdrop.

Opposite below left: Fish are a vital ingredient in pond design, helping to provide a balanced environment as well as constant movement. Varieties range from the common goldfish to the exotic Coy carp. Be sure to seek a specialist's advice before you make your final choice.

Opposite below right: Lily flowers are among the most spectacular in the garden and the great waxy blooms will bring high drama to any pool. Because their colors are so vibrant you should choose them to blend with the surrounding planting schemes.

Right: *An old glazed sink has been covered with Hypatufa, a mixture of cement, adhesive, and peat. This encourages the speedy growth of a layer of moss and lichen, mimicking the appearance of real stone and providing an interesting textured surface that blends well with the surrounding environment.*

Far right: *Half a barrel makes an excellent small pool, though it will be difficult to maintain an ecological balance to prevent stagnation if you are not prepared to clean and care for it regularly. The plants here are growing well but will need regular maintenance and thinning if they are not to overrun the area completely, becoming tangled and unrecognizable.*

SMALL-SCALE SOLUTIONS

Ponds can come in all shapes, sizes and containers, and need not necessarily be confined by conventional criteria. Having said that, the smaller the pool the more difficult it will be to maintain a balanced combination of plants and fish. Maintenance is often higher, particularly if fish are omitted, as unchecked weed and algae growth will need removing from time to time. It is worth remembering that even pools like this should not be completely emptied on a regular basis. You should drain off about a quarter of the water each year, which will remove a percentage of the toxins, and replace with fresh water. Replacing any more than that will upset the ecological balance that has built up.

In some instances you may not want a conventional pool at all. If young children use the garden, an area of open water will present a real hazard. An alternative would be to set an old millstone or drilled boulder above a tank and pump water up and over it in a continuous cycle. This recreates the refreshing sound of moving water, is irresistible to children and, most importantly, is completely safe. A raised bed could well incorporate this idea with planting, loose cobbles, and other boulders to complete the picture. Although a number of manufacturers produce simulated millstones, they rarely look as good as the real thing. A much better idea is to seek out just what you want, enjoying the satisfying knowledge that whatever you finally construct will be unique.

One water feature in my yard at home is a large cast-iron bath. It sits, ponderously, close to the french windows, surrounded by pots and containers of various sizes and is filled with water, fish, and plants. There is even a plug for easy drainage! It is the quickest pond I have ever built and looks just fine. For me the most important point is that I derived a great deal more pleasure from doing something constructive with the bath than I would have done if I had simply

Far left: *This pool has a Japanese feel but rather lacks conviction. Nonetheless, the idea of using cobbles as a beach is an excellent one and can be adapted to suit pools of varying styles. The stream of water flowing down the slate steps between the planting contributes a feeling of harmony and provides a relaxing "background noise" to peaceful activities.*

Left: *This is a real cracker of a stone sink, blending perfectly with the drystone wall and soft planting in a composition designed by Julian Dowle. Continuity and sensitivity have been blended into a harmonious whole—which is what good garden design is all about and which can be achieved with a combination of imagination and careful planning.*

broken it up and sent it down to the scrap yard.

Another eccentric pool I once designed was in an old boat. Again, this worked well, as a dinghy is equally equipped to keep water in as it is to keep it out. The composition was set in an informal part of the yard with the boat gently drifting out of a bed into the lawn. The inclusion of original and unexpected elements is one of the great strengths of good garden design—add humor to this and the picture is often complete.

Half a barrel filled with plants and water is a classic container for making into a small-scale pond. Make sure that the barrel did not previously contain wood preservative oil (the residue of which will contaminate the water), and scrub the inside of the barrel clean using water. Spread a layer of clean soil over the base of the barrel and mix with a little water to form mud. Bed a few pond plants in this mud, then add a layer of fine shingle above the soil to keep the plants rooted in place. Fill the barrel with water almost to the rim, taking care not to disturb the soil. You will need to let the water settle and allow the temperature to stabilize for about a week before adding a few fish and some snails.

Not all ponds need to be built as a single unit, however, and you could consider split-level arrangements where one plane of water drops to the next, either by a simple waterfall or a water slide of some kind. A variation of this idea is a water staircase where a series of ponds drop down a slope. Some of the great Italian Renaissance gardens featured such staircases on an enormous scale. Today, you could modify the idea and reduce it down to create a feature in a quite modest area. A sloping garden has perhaps the greatest potential for water which can be handled both formally and informally. A series of irregularly shaped pools linked by streams and falls and surrounded by planting will provide an entirely natural look, while crisply architectural sheets of water, worked into the angles of a flight of steps, create just the opposite effect. As long as the yard, or at least that part of the yard, embraces the overall theme, either approach would be entirely appropriate.

FOUNTAIN

Although water is one of the key elements in gardening, it can present problems. Safety is an obvious consideration and so, too, is maintenance to keep the surface clean. This feature presents a negligible hazard to children, is easy to build and looks delightful throughout the year. In addition, it provides a real focal point as well as a cooling influence on a hot summer's day. The relatively small scale demands that it be positioned close to a terrace or in full view of a window; otherwise it could all too easily be lost in a more distant part of the yard or concealed completely if poorly sited.

CONSTRUCTION

Strip the surface of the site of vegetation and mark a circle with a radius of 24in. (600mm) using a piece of string attached to a central stake to act as a compass. Carefully remove the topsoil within the circle to a depth of 3in. (75mm).

Mark a rectangle 18 × 24in. (450 × 600mm) within the center of the circle and dig this to a depth of 22in. (550mm), extending slightly beyond the edges of the rectangle. Position a layer of gravel, 3in. (75mm) thick, at the bottom of the pit, ram it down and cover the surface with sand to smooth out any irregularities. The tank to be placed in the pit, which can be made from either galvanized steel or plastic, can now be lowered into the pit and the position adjusted so that the base is level. Position a strip of butyl pond liner, approximately

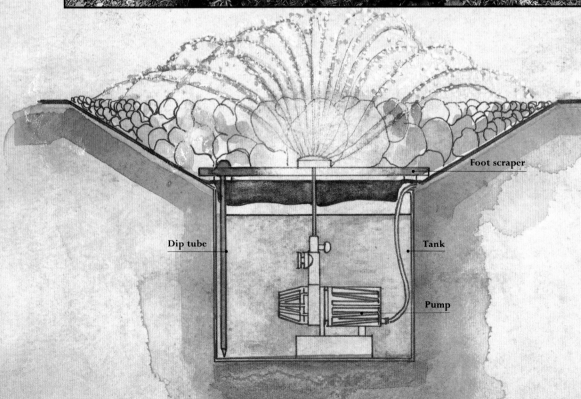

Foot scraper

Dip tube

Tank

Pump

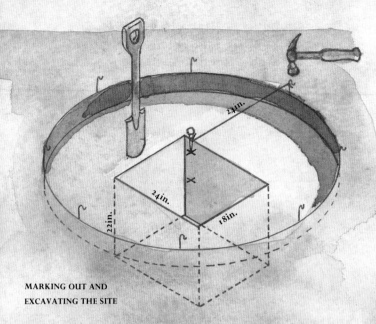

**MARKING OUT AND
EXCAVATING THE SITE**

12in. (300mm) wide, around the rim of the tank so that 6in. (150mm) hangs down on each side.

Carefully backfill soil around the tank, firming it down as you work. Grade the final slope up to the circumference of the surrounding circle, leaving two flat ledges, 3in. (75mm) wide, along the 24in. (600mm) long sides of the tank – these will support the foot-scrapers. Cover the soil surface with a thin layer of soft sand and fold the liner hanging on the inside of the tank back over the sand.

Cut another section of liner to form a circle 3in. (75mm) larger in diameter than that marked on the ground and cut a central hole 6in. (150mm) within the perimeter of the tank. When you have done this, carefully lay this liner in position.

The fountain is driven by a submersible, low-voltage pump fitted with a head that will finish just above the galvanized foot-scrapers. Choose one with an output of about 400gal./hr (30l/min). You can adjust the height of the pump

by standing it on bricks or concrete blocks built up within the tank. Run the cable from the pump over the liner. Use builders' tape to fasten and protect the cable at the point where it passes over the rim of the tank.

Two galvanized foot-scrapers are positioned on the prepared shelves (one on each side of the fountainhead) to keep loose boulders and pebbles from falling into the tank. Fit two scraps of doubled butyl pond liner over the shelves underneath the scrapers to act as cushions to the liner below.

During a hot summer, when the fountain is working, evaporation will be considerable. A dipstick is essential for regular checks to the water level within the tank. Cut a tube for the stick to run through from $\frac{3}{4}$in. (20mm) rigid plastic pipe to reach from the bottom of the tank to just above the level of the foot-scrapers. Position the pipe vertically and tie it to a slat on the scraper. Slide a bamboo cane down the tube and clearly mark on it one level 6in. (150mm) above the level of

the pump and another 3in. (75mm) below the rim of the tank; you can now use the cane to tell if the water level drops to a dangerous level and to check that you have topped up the tank with water to an appropriate level.

Use a hose to fill the tank so that the water level just covers the pump. Run the cable back to the house and connect it to the transformer according to the manufacturer's instructions. Any outside wiring must be carried out by a qualified electrician. Test the system and the pump for correct operation and adjust the fountain pressure for the

height of spray you want. There is normally a simple valve that you can easily adjust to achieve this.

Position loose stones and small, smooth boulders around the circumference of the circle, and trim off any excess pond liner that is visible. Position the remainder of the stones working from the center outward, so that the whole area is covered and there are no gaps through which you can see the pump mechanism in the tank below. Fill the tank to the upper mark on the dipstick, switch on the power to start the pump operating, and enjoy the results!

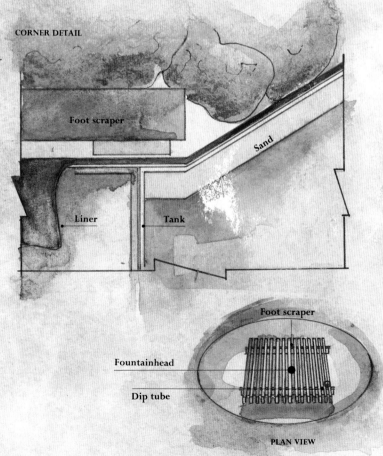

CORNER DETAIL

Foot scraper

Sand

Liner

Tank

Foot scraper

Fountainhead

Dip tube

PLAN VIEW

Above: Simplicity can achieve a great deal in visual terms. This concrete bowl is perfectly suited to its purpose as a birdbath. The tap is a practical idea and ensures that water is readily available.

Above right: An elaborate cast-iron or aluminium birdbath like this would be expensive, but is certainly elegant. Black is a good landscape color and blends well with planting, but such a shallow bath would need topping up regularly in hot weather.

BIRDBATHS AND FOUNTAINS

Birdbaths and fountains provide the finishing touches to your yard, the final details that put charisma into the composition. As well as being ecologically sound, allowing not just birds but many other wild creatures to drink, birdbaths act as pretty focal points, drawing the eye in a particular direction.

Shapes and styles of birdbaths vary enormously, from a basic wooden bowl set on the edge of a raised bed or wall to elaborate affairs cast in metal or hewn from stone. I believe that in all areas of design the simplest things work best and any feature should take its style from the area that surrounds it. The simplest birdbath might be a crevice set within a large rock, exactly right in an informal setting. The most complicated could be an ornate pattern in wrought-iron, perfectly at home in the formal setting of a crisp town garden while still fulfilling its function of attracting the local birdlife.

Birdbaths should be shallow and have gently sloping sides. If you or your neighbors have cats, then the birdbath should be set high enough to discourage cats from disturbing the birds. It is a good idea to line the bottom with coarse sand or gravel so that birds can get a foothold.

Fountains can be spectacular or simple, but must suit the overall yard pattern. A huge jet needs to be in a huge pond some distance from the house or viewing point, whereas a small fountain will do much the same visual job closer to home. The height at which the jet is set will also play a part. If it spouts from the top of a bowl at eye-level, much of the effect will be lost when sitting down. This would be a composition to be viewed when walking, perhaps in a front garden on the way to the main entrance. Similarly a bubble jet, just breaking the surface of the water, will be most effective when sitting. Think about height, position, and sound right at the beginning of the planning stages. It will certainly pay great dividends later on, when the fountain will be all the more appreciated if it can be seen to best advantage.

Left: *The delicious contrast between the formality of the fountain and the informality of the surrounding planting provides an excellent study in design. The pool is large enough to support both plants and a few small fish, while the arching sprays of water reflect the sunlight beautifully before falling past the bowl in the kind of shower that birds appreciate. Refreshing and pleasant to the eye and the ear, a fountain with a small pool is a welcome feature in any yard, and always contributes to a relaxing environment.*

DIRECTORY OF TECHNIQUES

LAYING A PATIO OF PAVING SLABS

Use pegs and string lines to mark out the area of the site according to the dimensions of the slabs so that, if possible, only whole slabs will be used. Allow for a consistent gap of $\frac{1}{4}-\frac{1}{2}$in. (6–12mm) between the slabs.

Excavate the site to a depth of 3–6in. (75–100mm) according to how firm the ground is (the firmer the ground, the shallower the excavation can be). Ram down a layer of hardcore in the bottom two thirds of your excavation, checking with a spirit level that the surface is flat and level. Cover the hardcore with a thin layer of sand to fill any gaps.

The concrete slabs should be laid on a continuous layer of mortar. It will be easier to bed the slabs on spots of mortar, however, on a sufficiently firm surface. Starting in one corner of the site, put down five spots of mortar, about $1\frac{1}{2}$–2in. (38–50mm) deep and 3in. (75mm) in diameter. Carefully align the slab with the string lines, and bed it on the mortar. Lay a short length of wood on the slab and tap down with a mallet until the slab is level. Use a spirit level to check that the crossfall and lengthways slope of the slab are even.

Using $\frac{1}{4}$in. (6mm) or $\frac{1}{2}$in. (12mm) plywood spacers, lay the first row of slabs, checking with a 3:4:5 triangle that the slabs are being laid square to the adjacent ones. You can make a 3:4:5 triangle from scrap wood: nail a 3in. (75mm) length at right angles to a 4in. (100mm) length, then nail a brace across the hypotenuse so that its length is exactly 5in. (125mm) from corner to corner.

Move the string line along to mark the outside edge of the second row of slabs, then lay the two slabs at either end, again using spacers. Fill in the remaining slabs, then repeat until you have paved the whole area.

Remove the spacers after two days, then fill in the gaps with mortar, or leave them open for grass to grow through.

LAYING A PATH

The hardest-wearing paths are laid on a continuous layer of mortar. Whether the surfacing material is stone, concrete slabs, crazy paving, or sections of hardwood, you should excavate the area just as for a patio, with a well-compacted layer of hardcore at the base. Again, bedding the material on generous spots of mortar is a simple task, and has the advantage of making it easier to lift them up should you need to reach any pipes buried beneath.

The simplest method, however, is to lay stepping stones across the lawn, setting them about $\frac{1}{2}$in. (12mm) below the level of the grass so that a mower can pass over.

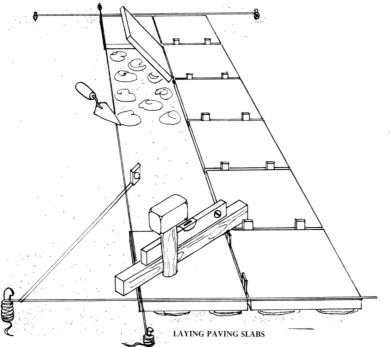

LAYING PAVING SLABS

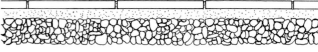

LAYING SLABS ON A LAYER OF MORTAR

LAYING SLABS ON SPOTS OF MORTAR

LAYING SLABS IN GRASS

STEPS FROM RAILROAD TIES

If the slope of the ground is not too steep, railroad ties can be recessed into the soil and pegged in place to provide an informal flight of steps in a yard. Dig out troughs: these should be to the length of the tie, and about ½in. (12mm) deep at the front and almost to the depth of the tie at the back. Ram the ties firmly in place and drive wooden stakes (thoroughly coated with non-toxic exterior-grade preservative) into the ground just in front of the sleepers to hold them in place. Place rocks between the treads for sculptural effect and grow plants at the sides to soften the edges.

For a slightly more formal and durable solution, railroad ties can be combined with concrete slabs. In this case, the ties and the slabs must be bedded on a 2in. (50mm) layer of mortar above a 6in. (150mm) layer of well-compacted hardcore, which means that you will have to excavate the site first. Bed the ties as shown (below) so that the top of the tie is level with the top of the slab "above" it. Tap the ties down with a mallet until they are level with the appropriate slabs, and check with a spirit level that the slabs themselves are not sloping. Take care that the tie does not protrude above the concrete slab, or someone may trip.

STEPS FROM BRICKS AND CONCRETE SLABS

The formal steps shown here are built up from ground level to a raised platform or patio of concrete slabs, rather than being built into an existing slope. They rest firmly in place above layers of hardcore, concrete, and mortar. This design might be useful if you want a hard-surfaced area above the patio area.

Measure the height difference between the upper and lower levels, and calculate how many treads (the concrete slabs) and risers (the bricks) you will require. Here, the small step only requires a riser from the ground level to the tread, and then requires a second riser going to the upper level.

Excavate according to the slope and lay well-compacted hardcore. Dig a trench 12in. (300mm) deep to support the first riser and fill it with about 1in. (25mm) of hardcore. Fill the rest of the trench with concrete, tamp it down flat, cover, and let it set for three days. Bed a row of bricks to the width of the step on a 2in. (50mm) layer of mortar, then lay a slab above it so that it protrudes beyond the riser by about 1in. (25mm). Ensure the tread is level, then bed the next row of risers. Repeat until the steps are the right height, always checking for horizontal.

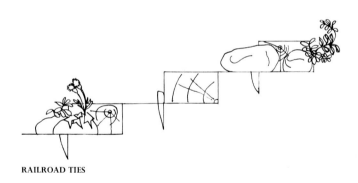

RAILROAD TIES

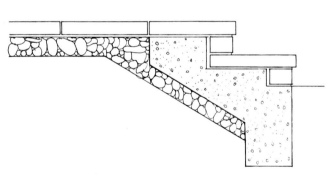

BRICKS AND CONCRETE SLABS

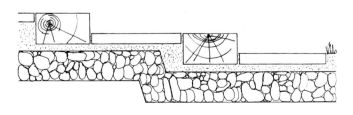

RAILROAD TIES AND CONCRETE SLABS

BUILDING A BRICK WALL

It is important to lay secure foundations when building a brick wall. Failure to do so will lead to rapid subsidence and collapse. The length and depth of foundations must vary according to the height of the construction; but if you are in doubt it is wise to be generous.

Anything higher than a low brick planter will need purpose-built, solid concrete foundations which should be twice the width of the wall. A single brick thickness wall, up to 39in. (1000mm) high, will require a trench 14–16in. (350–400mm) deep. Into this, lay a 6in. (150mm) deep level bed of concrete (one part cement to four parts ballast). The foundations then should be left to harden for four days and should be protected from the elements by covering in plastic during rain, or in damp sacking during hot weather. The sack should be sprayed with water to prevent the foundations cracking.

In addition to firm foundations, it is advisable to have piers (support columns) at both ends to ensure stability.

Once the foundations are ready, use string lines to act as a guide when you lay the first course of bricks. Set up profile boards with notches at the appropriate width for the wall either end of the trench and insert the string in the notches; this will hold it taut.

Next, spread a layer of mortar on the concrete bed. The mortar should be just over $\frac{3}{8}$in. (10mm) thick, bearing in mind that it will be compressed slightly by the application of the bricks. Set the first brick in place, indentation or "frog" upwards, at one end of the mortar. The next brick should be laid about 48in. (1220mm) away. To ensure that they are level, place a spirit level on a piece of wood bridging the two bricks and gently tap down the higher one with a trowel handle until they are level. Repeat for every brick in the first course, "buttering" each brick end with mortar to form the vertical joints.

Vertical joints must be staggered; the second course being started with a brick cut in half. To do this, cut a groove around a brick with a chisel and hammer, lay it on a bed of sand, insert the chisel in the groove, and tap sharply with the hammer to get a clean cut.

The ends of the wall should be built up three or four courses ahead of the course being completed. Each course must be laid to a taut string line, pinned into the course above the one you are laying.

As you build the wall you should check regularly with a length of wood marked with the height of each course that they are accurate, and that the face of the brickwork is even. As each course is completed, finish the joints by removing excess mortar with the edge of a trowel. These are known as flush joints. Rounded joints are achieved by rubbing back the mortar with a piece of hose or bucket handle. Lay the top course (the coping course) of bricks on edge to protect the wall from the worst of the weather.

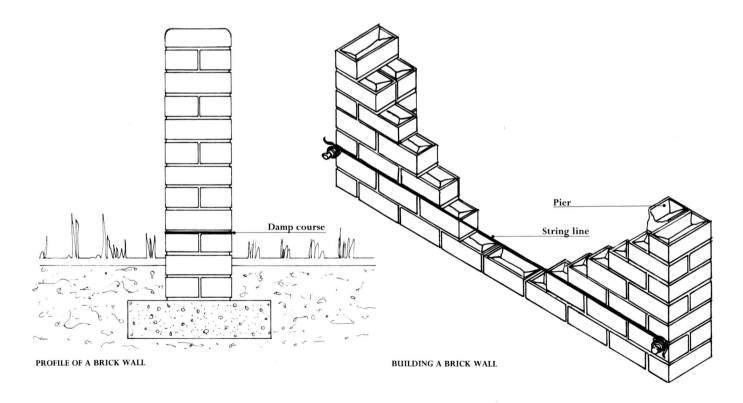

Damp course

Pier

String line

PROFILE OF A BRICK WALL

BUILDING A BRICK WALL

FIXING POSTS

Metal post spikes can be driven into soil and the post fitted into the square cup above the earth. Alternatively a posthole borer can be driven into the ground and then removed with the displaced earth. Fill the bottom of the hole with well-compacted hardcore, insert the post, and fill around with concrete, sloping it away from the post to allow better drainage.

On concrete or paving stones, you can use a steel base as the fixing point. The square plate can be bolted in place and the post inserted in the projecting cup. Alternatively, the bolt or bracket can be cemented into the paving and the post fitted into it. Another method is to chip through the surface of the patio or paving stones and then concrete the post in place without using a bracket. Always check the posts for vertical, adjust as necessary, and treat with non-toxic preservative.

FIXING TRELLIS PANELS

Trellis is often secured to walls, but an alternative, if this is not feasible or desirable, is to use vertical support posts. Having fastened these in the ground at the necessary distance apart (the spacing will depend on the width of the trellis of fence panels), place bricks or blocks on the ground to support the panels at the required height above the ground. To avoid the panels rotting at the bottom, trellis should be fixed at least 6in. (150mm) above ground level. Metal, purpose-made clips (panel brackets) can then be nailed into the posts at a suitable level. For panels up to 72in. (1800mm) high, you will require three clips per side. Ensure that the clips are at the same height on each post and inset by the same amount. Lift the panels into place, making sure that the horizontal rails of the panels are level. Fit the panels to the clips using zinc-plated or brass screws.

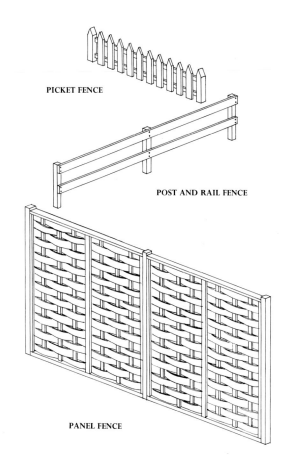

PICKET FENCE

POST AND RAIL FENCE

PANEL FENCE

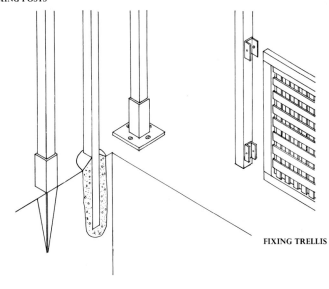

FIXING POSTS

FIXING TRELLIS

TYPES OF FENCING

The variety of styles of fencing mean that there is certain to be one that suits your needs perfectly.

Picket fences, with their pointed or rounded tops, are usually about 36in. (900mm) high, and are used to define a boundary, usually at the front of a house. Traditionally painted white, there's no reason why you shouldn't add a splash of color if the fancy takes you.

Post and rail fences definitely look best in a country setting, since they don't provide much in the way of privacy or protection, but do allow marvelous views of the scenery beyond. They are stock-proof, and gates should be of the five-bar type. Alternatively, you can build stairs that will allow you to cross over the fence with ease.

Panel fences are quite expensive, especially if your boundary is quite large, but they are easy to install. They provide the best degree of privacy and weather protection, although used at the front of the house they look rather hostile. A large expanse of panel fence is not the most attractive of sights: the best thing is to plant some fast-growing climbers against the panel to provide a more attractive view.

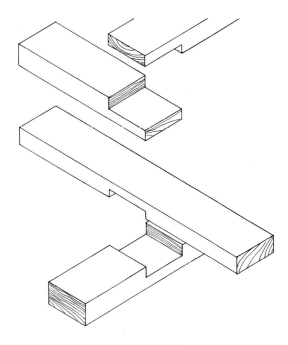

ABOVE: END-LAP JOINT; BELOW: "X" HALF-LAP JOINT

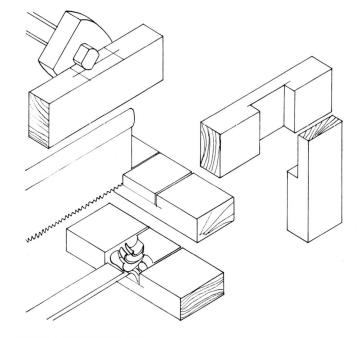

CUTTING A "T" HALF-LAP JOINT

WOOD JOINTS

In order to ensure that anything you build in the yard is strong and secure, it is essential that you join various pieces of work accurately. The joints described here will be useful in building many of the projects featured in this book. Although it is important to measure the dimensions accurately, don't be deterred by striving for an absolutely perfect finish: one of the joys of building wooden structures in the yard is that they will mellow with age, and will often have plants growing up and around them. For this reason, the quality of the finish does not need to be as fine as if you were making a piece of furniture for use indoors. However, it is a good idea to practice cutting joints on some pieces of scrap wood first.

CUTTING A BUTT JOINT

This is the simplest woodworking joint of all. The edge of one piece of wood is butted up against the side or face of another piece of wood, and fastened in place with glue. The joint is normally further reinforced using nails or corrugated fasteners.

It is important that the faces of the pieces of wood to be joined are cut or planed square so that they butt together neatly.

A variation on the butt joint is the miter joint, in which the edges or faces of the two pieces of wood to be joined are cut at an angle and then butted together. Usually, the angle is cut at 45 degrees, so that the pieces of wood form a right angle when joined. However, they can be cut to any angle, as is the case with the fascia boards for the arbor project.

CUTTING A HALF-LAP JOINT

Half-lap joints are used to join two pieces of wood of similar dimensions. The joint requires both pieces of wood to be cut through half their thickness (hence the name). There are three variations of the joint, according to where the two pieces of wood are being jointed: an end lap joint joins two pieces of wood at their ends; a "T" half-lap joint joins the end of one board to a point anywhere along the length of the other piece of wood; and an "X" half-lap joint is formed when the faces of two pieces of wood are jointed to meet along their lengths.

Mark on each piece of wood the width of the cut-out (that is, the width of the other piece of wood), using a try square to make sure that it is square. Transfer the

lines of the cut-out to the edges of the wood and, with a marking gauge, set to half the thickness of the piece of wood, mark the depth of the cut-out. Hold the piece of work in a vise and, using a back saw, carefully cut down the marked lines to the depth of the joint (half the thickness of the piece of wood), then carefully chisel out the waste wood.

If you are sawing an end-lap joint, then you will be measuring in for the thickness of the joint from the end of the piece of wood. In this case, first cut down the marked line to the depth of the joint; next, turn the piece of wood on end (so that it is upright) and replace it firmly in the vise. You can now carefully saw down the length of the joint, again using a back saw. Any rough edges can be sanded.

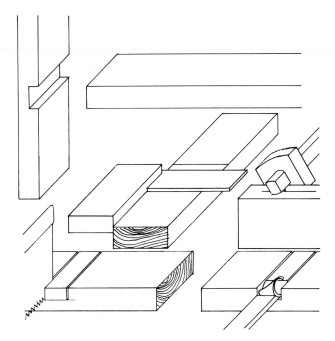

CUTTING A DADO JOINT

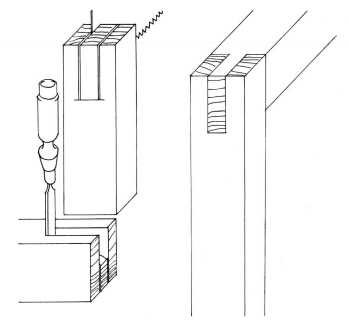

CUTTING A NOTCH JOINT

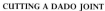

CUTTING A DADO JOINT

A dado (groove) joint is essentially a slot into which the end of a piece of wood fits at right angles.

Mark the width of the slot (that is, the width of the piece of wood that will be joined) across the wide face of the piece of wood into which it will be cut. Use a try square for this, and extend the lines over onto the edges of the piece of wood.

The slot should be cut to a depth that is half the thickness of the piece of wood. Use a marking gauge to mark the depth between the marked lines on the edges.

Score across the lines marking the width of the slot so that you can locate the blade of the saw more easily, and cut down to the depth of the joint using a back saw. Chisel out the waste wood, working in from both edges.

CUTTING A RABBET AND DADO JOINT

This is used to join the corners of a frame, and is very strong because a rabbet in the corner of one piece of wood is held in the dado (groove) cut into the other piece. When cutting this joint, the end of the piece of wood in which the dado is cut should be left overlong; the excess wood is then cut off neatly, flush with the top of the joint once the tongue has been nailed in place.

Mark out and cut the dado to a depth of between one third and half the thickness of the wood. On the other piece, mark out a rabbet so that it will fit snugly in the dado. The rabbet should be no less than half the wood's thickness. Join the two pieces so the rabbet is on the underside of the corner.

CUTTING A NOTCH JOINT

A notch joint is like a mortise and tenon joint, except that the mortise (slot) is cut in the top of one of the pieces of wood into which the tenon (tongue) fits.

Mark out the tenon centrally on the end of one of the pieces of wood to about one third the thickness of the wood. The length of the tenon should be the width of the other piece of wood. Mark this distance down from the end and square the line around all four faces. Use a back saw to cut down the length of the tongue, then saw across the sides to remove the rest of the waste.

Mark the width of the slot on the end of the other piece of wood to correspond to the width of the tenon. Use a back saw to cut down to the depth of the slot, then neatly chisel out the waste.

CUTTING A RABBET

A rabbet is an L-shaped cut along the end or edge of a piece of wood to accommodate another piece at right angles to it. Sometimes, a rabbet is cut in both pieces so that they slot together.

Mark the rabbet along the end or length of the piece of wood. Its width should be the thickness of the piece of wood that is going to be joined to it; its depth should not exceed half of the width. If you are cutting rabbets in both pieces of wood, their width and depth should be half the thickness of the wood.

Clamp the piece of wood and cut down to the width of the rabbet using a back saw. Lay the piece of wood down flat and cut down to the depth of the rabbet. If the rabbet is very shallow, you may prefer to chisel out the waste.

INDEX

ACKNOWLEDGMENTS

The publisher thanks the following photographers and organisations for their permission to reproduce the pictures in this book:

1 Yves Duronsoy; 2–3 background Brigitte Thomas; 2 above left Jerry Harpur (designer Christopher Masson); 2 above right Ron Sutherland/ Garden Picture Library; 2 below left Karen Bussolini; 2 below right Ron Sutherland/Garden Picture Library; 4 left Karen Bussolini; 4 center Friedrich Strauss (Horst Schummelfeder); 4 right Edifice/Lewis; 4–5 Michael Boys/Boys Syndication; 5 left Karen Bussolini; 5 center S&O Mathews; 5 right Michael Boys/Boys Syndication; 6–7 Camera Press; 8 Jerry Harpur (designer Michael Balston); 9 Brigitte Thomas (Erwan Tymen); 10–11 Brigitte Thomas (Erwan Tymen); 11 Jerry Harpur/Conran Octopus (architect John Burgee, garden Gwen Burgee with Tim Du Val); 12–13 Karen Bussolini; 13 Linda Burgess/Insight Picture Library; 14 Jerry Harpur (designer Ernie Taylor/Great Barr. West Midlands); 15 S&O Mathews; 16–17 Michael Boys/Boys Syndication; 18 Brigitte Thomas/ Garden Picture Library; 19 Friedrich Strauss (Horst Schummelfeder); 20–21 background Linda Burgess/Insight Picture Library; 20 above left Jerry Harpur (designer Arabella Lennox-Boyd); 20 above right Jerry Harpur (designers Julie Toll & John Chambers. R.H.S. Chelsea 1991); 20 below left Jerry Harpur (Hazleby House, Berkshire); 20 below right Jerry Harpur/Conran Octopus; 22 above Jerry Harpur (designer Tim Newbury for Cramphorns P.L.C. R.H.S. Chelsea 1991); 22 below Karen Bussolini; 23 Jerry Harpur (designer Hilary McMahon. Costins Nursery. R.H.S. Chelsea 1991); 24–25 background Friedrich Strauss; 25 above left Jerry Harpur (designer Bruce Kelly, New York); 25 above right Friedrich Strauss (Horst Schummelfeder); 25 below S&O Mathews; 26 Jerry Harpur ("Dolwen" Llanrhaedr-ym-Mochnant); 27 Ron Sutherland/Garden Picture Library; 28 Eric Crichton; 30 Christopher Sykes; 30 right Brigitte Thomas (Timothy Vaughan); 31 above Jerry Harpur/Conran Octopus; 31 below Jerry Harpur (designer Ann Alexander Sinclair); 32 left Karen Bussolini; 32 above right Brigitte Thomas (Diana Humelen); 32 below right Ron Sutherland/Garden Picture Library; 33 above Friedrich Strauss (Horst Schummelfeder); 33 below Karen Bussolini; 34 Karen Bussolini; 36–37 Brigitte Thomas (Walda Pairon); 38 Andrew Lawson; 39 Michael Boys/Boys Syndication; 40 above Jerry Harpur ("Dolwen" Llanrhaedr-ym-Mochnant); 40 below Brigitte Thomas; 40–41 Friedrich Strauss (Horst Schummelfeder); 42 John Heseltine; 46 Andrew Lawson; 47 above John Glover/Garden Picture Library; 47 below Hugh Palmer; 48 Jerry Harpur; 52–53 Michael Boys/Boys Syndication; 54 left S&O Mathews; 54 right S&O Mathews; 55 left Christopher Sykes; 55 right Jerry Harpur/Conran Octopus (architect John Burgee, garden Gwen Burgee with Tim Du Val); 56–57 background Andrew Lawson; 56 above left Hugh Palmer; 56 above right John Ferris; 56 below left Karen Bussolini; 56 below right Brigitte Thomas (Erwan Tymen); 58–59 Jean-Paul Bonhommet; 59 above Jerry Harpur/Conran Octopus; 59 below John Heseltine; 60 Friedrich Strauss; 62 Jerry Harpur/Elizabeth Whiting & Associates (Gail Jenkins. Melbourne); 63 S&O Mathews; 64 Ron Sutherland/Garden Picture Library; 66 above left Jerry Harpur (designer Douglas Knight/Formby Lancashire); 66 above right Eric Crichton (Peter Aldington); 66 below Friedrich Strauss; 67 S&O Mathews; 68 Edifice/Lewis; 69 above Peter Woloszynski; 69 below Jerry Harpur/Elizabeth Whiting & Associates (Sir Peter & Lady Finley. Sydney.); 70–71 Richard Bryant/Arcaid; 72 Jerry Harpur (Lower Hall Worfield/Salop, designed by Lanning Roper); 73 Ron Sutherland/Garden Picture Library; 74 above Friedrich Strauss (Horst Schummelfeder); 74 below Linda Burgess/Insight; 75 above David Russell/Garden Picture Library; 75 below John Miller; 76 above Friedrich Strauss (Landscape architect Neuberger); 76 below John Miller; 77 S&O Mathews; 78 Ron Sutherland/Garden Picture Library; 80–81 background Robert O'Dea; 81 above left John Miller; 81 below left Michael Boys/Boys Syndication; 81 above right Jack Townsend/Insight; 81 below right Michael Boys/Boys Syndication; 82 left Ron Sutherland/Garden Picture Library; 82 right Steven Wooster/Garden Picture Library; 83 left Jerry Harpur (designer Keith Gott, Japanese Garden Co. R.H.S. Chelsea 1991); 83 right Ron Sutherland/Garden Picture Library; 84 Eric Crichton (Mrs Fuller); 86 Ron Sutherland/Garden Picture Library; 87 Linda Burgess/Insight Picture Library.